DRY SUIT
DIVING
A GUIDE TO DIVING DRY

ID0947897

by Steve Barsky, Dick Long, and Bob Stinton
Forward by Sir John Rawlins

STORY ORIGINS

1. *The Fellowship of the Ring* by J.R.R. Tolkien; *Outward Bound* by Sutton Vane

2. "The Landlady" by Roald Dahl

3. *The Adventures of Marco Polo*, Richard J. Walsh ed.

4. "The Secret Lover" by Peter Lovesey

5. "Mr. Bearstowe Says" by Anthony Berkeley

6. *Three Dialogues Between Hylas and Philonous* by George Berkeley

7. "In the Fog" by Richard Harding Davis

8. "Exclusive report: Occupy Movement's 'Black Bloc' anarchists Demand Government Handouts" by Kyle Becker http://www.conservativedailynews.com/2012/04/exclusive-report-occupy-movements-black-bloc-anarchists-demand-government-handouts/

9. "Mr. Loveday's Little Outing" by Evelyn Waugh

MASTER POINT PRESS
ON THE INTERNET

www.masterpointpress.com

Our main site, with information about our books and software, reviews and more.

www.teachbridge.com

Our site for bridge teachers and students—free downloadable support material for our books, helpful articles, forums and more.

www.bridgeblogging.com

Read and comment on regular articles from MPP authors and other bridge notables.

www.ebooksbridge.com

Purchase downloadable electronic versions of MPP books and software.

DRY SUIT DIVING
A GUIDE TO DIVING DRY

by Steve Barsky, Dick Long, and Bob Stinton
Forward by Sir John Rawlins

Watersport Publishing, Inc.
Post Office Box 83727
San Diego, CA 92138

Disclaimer

Scuba diving is a potentially hazardous practice and if practiced incorrectly or with incomplete planning and procedures can expose a person to considerable risks including serious injury or even death. It requires specialized training, equipment and experience. This book is not intended as a substitute for the above or for the diver to abandon common sense in pursuit of diving activities which are beyond his abilities. This book is intended as a source of information on various aspects of dry suit diving, not as a substitute for proper supervised training and experience. For training in dry suit diving, contact a national certification agency. The reader is advised that all the elements of hazard and risk associated with scuba diving and using dry suits cannot be brought out within the scope of this text. The authors, publisher, and manufacturers presented in this book, are not liable for damage or injury including death which may result from any scuba diving activities, with respect to information contained herein.

Photography by Steve Barsky, except as noted.
Design and typography by Watersport Publishing, Inc.
Cover Design by Theresa Lambert

First Printing 1992
Watersport Publishing, Inc., P.O. Box 83727, San Diego, CA 92138

Printed in the United States

International Standard Book Number
ISBN 0-922769-36-2

Library of Congress Catalog Card Number: 91-67890
Barsky, Steve, Long, Dick, Stinton, Bob
Dry Suit Diving
A Guide To Diving Dry

4

Table of Contents

Acknowledgements

Nothing is ever as easy as it sounds, and that includes producing a book. It's not just the writing, but all of the other aspects of the book that make it successful. For a book like this one, those other aspects included rounding up the equipment, working with boat operators and models, shipping the gear back to the manufacturers, verifying technical information, shooting the photos, editing, layout, and production. Without the encouragement and cooperation of many people, this book would never have happened.

First and foremost we would like to thank Ken Loyst and the staff at Watersport Publishing, Inc. Ken appreciated the value of this project and did not hesitate to endorse it from the very beginning.

Many manufacturers have assisted us by providing equipment and photographs. Norma Ockwig and John Ennis at Amron made available both Nokia suits and photographs. Phil Joy at Gates provided many photos of their production facilities. Claude Rorabaugh at Harvey's furnished us with photos of their suits. Charlotte Rosen at Poseidon tracked down fascinating historical photos of early Unisuits. Sue Anne Griffin at O'Neill also furnished us with early photos of Jack O'Neill. Shirley Richards at 3M provided technical information and photographs of their Thinsulate® material. Mike Brock at Whites Scubapro Ltd. supplied photos of their suits and undergarments. Stig Insulan of S.I. Tech assisted us with historical photos from his early days of diving. The staff at Diving Unlimited International, Inc. bent over backwards to make sure we had the gear we needed for photos at the right time.

Special thanks to Judy Brody at the Cousteau Society for researching and supplying the early photo of Jacques Cousteau. The society is a member supported, non-profit environmental organization and we appreciate their assistance.

Photographers who have generously contributed their photographs include Kristine Barsky, Bob Cranston, Ronnie Damico, Eric Hanauer, John Heine, Dennis Osterlund, and Bev Morgan. Bev also took the time to read the chapter on the history of thermal protection and shared many valuable insights on the early days of diving.

Many of our friends and dive buddies appear in the book and helped us get the photos that make this book special. They include Jerry Clouser, Ronnie Damico, Gary Davis, Ingvar Elfstrom, Dave Forcucci, John Heine,

Dave Hubbard, Stig Insulan, Bob Meistrell, Bill Meistrell, Steve Mitchell, Dan Richards, Ron Russell, Carol Stewart, and John Trone. In particular, thanks to Bob Evans for taking us diving and giving us the opportunity to work off his boat.

Across the sea, Sir John Rawlins, retired Royal Navy doctor, and Nick Baker, secretary of the Historical Diving Society, gave us a great deal of assistance. Sir John enlightened us on historical diving practices from the Royal Navy, while Nick was able to secure photos from the Siebe Gorman archives.

John Wozny also reviewed the manuscript and made many valuable suggestions for improvement. His help and friendship are always treasured.

The principle model for the book was Kristine Barsky, who once again sacrificed days of her personal time to assist with this project. She modeled for most of the photos in the book and made many dives to ensure we got the best photos possible. In addition, Kristine spent hours editing and verifying information for us. There is no way we could have completed this project without her cooperation and interest.

September 1991
Steve Barsky, Dick Long and Bob Stinton

Foreword: Sir John Rawlins

In the winter of 1956 I was trained as a Royal Navy Shallow Water Diver in Great Britain. We used closed-circuit oxygen and semi-closed circuit nitrox breathing apparatus and wore neck entry dry suits. The dry suits then were made of rubber coated nylon over a cotton undersuit. Wetsuits were unavailable to us at that time.

The dry suit system we used seemed to work well, provided the dives we made were relatively short and shallow. Aside from the chill we experienced from diving in cold water, almost all of our operations were conducted from inflatable boats. If you didn't get cold during the dive, the chill you experienced during the ride back to shore was enough to make most divers hypothermic. However, in those days, the training was tough and divers were expected to be tough, too. If you complained about the cold you could be expected to be dropped from the course, so nobody mentioned their discomfort.

Diving below 60 feet with these dry suits was very uncomfortable. The pressure caused the suit to compress around the diver in tight folds that pinched the skin and caused welts. One suit in particular, that always fit loosely in the crotch, could be suddenly and startlingly painful if the diver went below 70 feet!

Long before suit inflation systems became common, my dive team and I experimented with a suit inflation system. We used a small high pressure cylinder carried in a pouch on the thigh, and used various gases including air, CO_2, and Freon. We vented the gas from our suits during ascent by slipping a finger under the flexible seals at the neck or wrists. There were occasional problems such as rapid uncontrolled ascents due to accidental over-inflation and occasional partial flooding. Fortunately, due to the extensive training our Royal Navy divers received, no casualties resulted from these potentially disastrous incidents.

This same dry suit system I had used back in 1956 was still in service in 1965, when we conducted a detailed physiological study of thermal effects of diving in cold water. Oral temperatures were recorded on 15 trainee divers when the water temperature was 40 degrees F. After 30-40 minute long dives, when temperatures were taken 5 minutes after exiting the water, the divers' temperatures ranged from 96.5 to 88.6 degrees F. In 8 of the trainees the temperatures were below 93 degrees F and in 5 it was 91 degrees F or less.

The colder men exhibited symptoms of nausea, lightheadedness, and headache. One of them had signs of early cold injury in one hand. He collapsed and had to be pulled from the water. Another trainee also collapsed and lost consciousness.

These observations highlighted the dangers of hypothermia in diving, the rapidity of its onset, and its unpredictability resulting from individual diver's reactions in response to cold. It was obvious that if hypothermic collapse took place outside of a training situation the outlook for the diver wasn't good.

The introduction of the foam neoprene wetsuit was received enthusiastically by the Royal Navy divers. The suits were easy to get into, they were comfortable, and they looked good. The story that they worked by preserving a layer of warm water around the diver was accepted without question. It quickly became obvious, though, that this warm layer inside the suit represented heat loss from the surface of the diver's skin. It also became apparent that the diver would remain warm only as long as the diver's metabolism could enable a heat gradient to be maintained across the warm layer and the suit material to the surrounding water.

It didn't take us too long to learn that for long or deep dives, wetsuits were very inferior to dry suits. By that time, dry suits were available with standard suit inflation systems and valves.

In 1967 I rode in a wet sub at 3 knots during a test dive wearing a dry suit with a proper suit inflation system. The designer of the vehicle wore a wetsuit, and exhausted his semi-closed circuit nitrox breathing apparatus in 30 minutes. The speed of the sub forced cold water through his suit, increasing his breathing rate, causing him to run through his breathing supply rapidly. He was forced to surface while I had the fun of driving the sub back to base underwater, quite warm and with breathing gas to spare. It was a valuable lesson.

In 1968, I joined the U.S. Navy's Sea Lab III project as part of the thermal protection division. The scientist who had worked on the project before me had shown that even when divers wore 4 layers of 1/4 inch foam neoprene they could not maintain thermal balance in 40 degree F water. Some form of heat replacement for the diver was essential. A dry suit with an undersuit heating system was the obvious solution, but U.S. Navy policy did not allow dry suits to be used at that time.

Wetsuits had several major disadvantages for the SeaLab habitat that was scheduled to be placed at 600 feet. First, a foam neoprene suit would compress to about half of its original thickness when taken to 600 feet. It took 120 hours for the suit to expand back to 65% of its original thickness, as the helium in the underwater habitat diffused into the cells of the material. In addition, since the thermal conductivity of helium is 6 times that of air, the insulation value of the suit at depth was about half the normal value. Finally, when the diver entered the water, the helium rapidly diffused out of the neoprene and the suit collapsed again.

The most significant disadvantage of the wetsuits, however, was the flushing of cold water in and out of the suit with the diver's movements. Even breathing caused this effect. We observed that when divers worked hard, heat loss almost doubled!

The decision to use wetsuits in Sea Lab III proved disastrous. When the habitat was placed on the bottom at 600 feet it leaked heavily, and two divers were sent down to try to stop the leaks. With an air temperature of 56 degrees F and water temperature of 47 degrees F it took the divers two hours to transfer from normal atmospheric breathing air to an atmosphere of 98% helium and 2% oxygen via the diving bell to the bottom. The divers became so chilled that they reported that entering the water felt "like stepping into a hot bath". Within minutes they were shivering uncontrollably and felt they were not getting enough gas to breathe. The dive was aborted.

Seven hours later they were prepared to try again, although there was no means of knowing to what extent they had managed to rewarm. The procedure was as before, but after only 4 minutes in the water one of the divers collapsed and lost consciousness. By the time he was recovered into the bell he was dead.

The Board of Inquiry attributed his death to improperly prepared breathing gear. I examined the set myself and I am not convinced. As we have seen above, hypothermia alone could have accounted for his collapse; certainly it must have played a major part.

Hypothermia is a killer. Divers have been shown to be incapable of accurately judging their own thermal state. There is no reason for a diver to expose himself to these dangers today now that we have dry suits that do not leak and that are fitted with reliable valves. Insulation materials are available with properties that were unobtainable in 1960.

For the serious sport diver today, the dry suit offers the best protection against cold and significantly reduces the chances of suffering from decompression sickness. Safe and efficient use of a dry suit, as with all diving equipment, requires good training, good discipline, and good practice. That is what this unique book is all about.

Sir John Rawlins
Surgeon Vice Admiral, Royal Navy

Chapter 1

A Brief History of Diver Thermal Protection

The main limiting factor in man's ability to go underwater has always been the ability to keep the diver warm. Given an unlimited air supply and the proper facilities for decompression, a diver could, theoretically, stay underwater for many hours. But without the right thermal protection, most divers will become chilled and inefficient even in relatively warm water.

Divers have experimented with many ways to stay warm. As materials, technology, and insulation have changed, diving suits have become more rugged and warmer. However, the basic principles of human physiology, insulation, and heat loss have not changed. Each new dive suit design represents another attempt to solve these problems.

Heavy Gear

In 1837, Augustus Siebe, an Englishman, developed the closed diving "dress" that connected to the diving helmet he had invented. This equipment was originally developed for commercial divers who worked on the bridges, piers, and wharfs throughout Great Britain.

The closed dress was originally developed to allow the diver to bend at the waist, without losing air out of the bottom of his helmet. The suit was made of waterproofed canvas. With the closed dress attached to the base of the helmet, the diver was completely isolated from the water, except for his hands. The side benefit to this was that the diver's body was kept dry. Long underwear, or even clothing, could be worn under the dress to keep the diver warm. Siebe's dress was the first "dry suit".

A heavy gear helmet designed by Bev Morgan and Bob Kirby in the early 1960's. The air inlet valve is just below the face port on the diver's left. The exhaust valve is located on the back of the helmet and could be operated by hand or from inside the helmet with the diver's head.

photo by Bev Morgan

Jacques Cousteau in an early dry suit.

photo Courtesy by The Cousteau Society.

Siebe's dress was a *passive insulation system*, with no external energy supplied to keep the diver warm. The suit worked because it trapped a layer of air between the diver's body and the external water environment.

Although Siebe's first helmet was not equipped with valves, the helmets he developed later featured both inlet and exhaust valves. The valves allowed the diver to precisely control his buoyancy.

This equipment has been known as deep sea diving gear, commercial gear, or heavy gear. Over the years, many different inventors developed new heavy gear designs, but the basic principles of this type of equipment have remained unchanged. This type of equipment is still in use in some parts of the world today.

World War II

Just prior to World War II, in 1938, recreational diving was limited to a small but dedicated group of enthusiasts in the Mediterranean. Among these divers was Jacques Cousteau, who built an early dry suit for scuba diving from vulcanized rubber. The suit had no valves or means of pressure equalization.

During World War II naval operations reached a scope and sophistication not previously seen. There were more and larger ships with greater firepower than in the past. Diving became more important than ever before as a means of salvage and for combat purposes. The term "frogman" was born during this era to describe combat divers using various types of diving equipment.

Both the British and the Italians worked very hard at developing "midget" submarines that could carry one or more divers. These tiny submersibles were known as "wet subs" and were very similar in concept to some of the sport diving submarines still seen today. The main purpose of

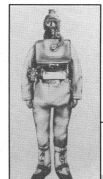

A U.S. Army Special Forces diver pauses during a training exercise. Note the dry suit and dry bag for transporting radios and other equipment.

photo courtesy of the Siebe Gorman Collection.

the wet subs was to carry a team of divers into an enemy harbor, undetected, so that explosives could be placed on the hulls of warships.

The divers who rode these subs wore closed diving suits and closed circuit rebreathers. The suits were not much different from those worn with traditional heavy gear. They were bulky and heavy, making it difficult to swim. The closed circuit rebreather is a type of breathing apparatus that recirculates the diver's exhaled breath, purifies it, and emits no bubbles.

Most of the work that was done to develop diving equipment during this time was performed by Sir Robert H. Davis, who worked at Siebe, Gorman & Company in Surrey, England. Davis was a famous diving inventor who wrote the classic book, *Deep Diving and Submarine Operations.*

Davis describes in detail some of the tests that were conducted to see if the divers could function in the 45 degree F water for the long sub rides into enemy waters. At that time, it was hard to find materials that would keep the divers warm, yet allow the divers to swim. Electrically heated suits were considered, but the idea was abandoned since the divers had to leave the sub to attach the explosives to the ships. In all probability, neither battery technology or materials technology were developed to the point that this would have been possible during this period.

The British Navy ultimately settled on silk underwear next to the diver's skin, woolen underwear on top of that, and kapok padded shirts and pants for the top layer. However, the major problem remained the diver's hands and no satisfactory solution was developed. Davis mentions that some divers actually went bare-handed with only a thick coating of grease to protect them! The divers referred to one version of the dry suits as the "clammy death"...

In 1946, Cousteau developed the constant volume dry suit. To get air into the suit, the diver blew air past the seal of his mask into the hood of the suit. The suit was equipped with exhaust valves on the head, wrist, and ankles, so air could be vented in any position.

Dry Suits and Wetsuits in the 1950's

After World War II, sport diving became popular in the United States. Some of the elements that contributed to this growth were movies like *The Frogmen*, the Cousteau book and film of *The Silent World*, and the appearance of *Skindiver* magazine in 1951. Also, there was a great deal of surplus military diving equipment on the market that had not been previously available.

Dry suits were the only type of effective thermal protection available for the sport diver during this period. As with all diving suits, even today, one of the major problems has always been how to get into the suit. The method of entry, whether by zipper or other device, always affects the fit and much of the performance of the suit.

Early dry suits had three means of entry. One design was known as a tunnel entry suit, another was via a split seal at the waist, and the third was through the neck seal.

Tunnel entry suits had a large tube located on the chest or upper back of the suit. The diver stuck his legs into the lower part of the suit, then pulled the top on over his head and arms. The tube or "tunnel" was then twisted closed and sealed with a clamp or rubber tubing.

Waist entry suits were equipped with a separate set of pants and jacket. They were made in Italy by Pirelli (the same people who make tires today). Both pieces came with excess material at the waist. This material was then folded together over a hard rubber cummerbund to create an effective seal. A large, heavy duty O-ring squeezed the folded layers against the cummerbund.

Neck entry suits were one piece suits similar in design to the dry suits available today, but without a zipper. The top of the suit had an opening large enough for the diver to stretch over his entire body. The latex neck seal was a separate piece. A metal ring fit closely over the diver's head and was worn around the neck. The rubber at the suit opening overlapped the bottom of the neck seal rubber. A metal clamp was placed over this effecting a seal.

Dry suit manufacturers during this period included Aquala, So-Lo Marx Rubber Co., Healthways, Pirelli, and Bel Aqua. There were four major drawbacks to dry suits at this time. First, none of the suit entry methods made it easy to use a dry suit. Second, the low pressure inflator mechanism had yet to be invented. Without this device, there was no way to equalize pressure inside the suit to adjust buoyancy or prevent suit squeeze. Third, the materials available to build dry suits were not as rugged or reliable as those

This diver is wearing an Aquala tunnel entry suit with a Scott Hydropak.

available today. Finally, the insulation materials available, such as wool, did not perform as well as the insulators we have today.

Dr. Hugh Bradner, a physicist, developed the first wetsuits in 1952, although he first wrote up the concept in 1951. In a memo of June 21, 1951 Bradner wrote,

"Actually, I do not think it is necessary to have a waterproof suit. It would be possible to obtain adequate warmth by use of a dead water space from a furry type of porous material. ...a two piece suit and zipper would be desirable though there is no need in this design for a waterproof zipper.

Another design might be a sponge rubber suit which would only have to be 1/4" thick."

Bradner set up two small companies to build suits for the Navy Underwater Demolition Teams (UDT) frogmen, but withdrew from the business after a short time. He also applied for a patent but never followed through on the issue.

Bev Morgan, a lifeguard and diver in Los Angeles County, developed the first commercially successful wetsuits in 1953. He sold the suits through his store, Dive 'n Surf in Redondo Beach. The suits were made from foam neoprene rubber and had no nylon lining. The wetsuit, as most divers know, traps a thin layer of water that is warmed by the diver's body. The insulation is in the gas bubbles trapped within the foam neoprene. The wetsuit is another example of passive insulation.

Dick Long in an early wetsuit.

The wetsuit quickly became more popular than the dry suit. Wetsuits have a number of advantages over dry suits for dives in moderate water temperatures. Wetsuits represent a relatively inexpensive initial investment compared to dry suits. Wetsuits also require less maintenance and less training than dry suits. However, for dives in water colder than 65 degrees, deep dives, multiple dives at moderate temperatures, or extended dives the wetsuit does not offer the best thermal protection.

The dry suit steadily lost popularity until new technology became available. Meanwhile divers were experimenting with other methods of keeping warm.

Diving in the 60's - Active Insulation and the Unisuit

Manned exploration of the oceans increased at an incredible rate during the 1960's. The combined effect of scientific exploration, technological development, and industrial progress all pushed diving technology rapidly forward.

From a scientific perspective, this was the era where it was proposed that man would colonize the seas and live underwater. Many different underwater habitats were built and placed on the bottom of the ocean. The Cousteau group built Conshelf Two which sat on the bottom of the Red Sea at a depth of 33 feet in 1963.

In 1964 the U.S. Navy placed the SEALAB I habitat at 193 feet off Bermuda. Four men lived underwater for 11 days. The Navy followed this with SEALAB II at a depth of 205 feet off La Jolla, California, in 1965. Three ten man teams spent two weeks on the bottom during this project. The water temperature ranged from 46 to 50 degrees F.

Dick Long built wetsuits for the SEALAB II divers per the Navy's orders, but the suits could not keep the divers warm at that depth. Long had been a diving instructor and inventor for many years. He had built many suits for the Navy by the time the SEALAB project took place, but none that had been required to work under such demanding conditions.

Suit compression, water temperature, and the use of helium as a breathing mixture all contributed to making the wetsuits very ineffective during SEALAB II. The following remark by one of the divers is typical of the reactions to the water temperature during SEALAB II.

A non-compressible wetsuit developed for the Navy by 3M Corporation.

"I won't say it got unbearable - it wouldn't be to the point that if an emergency arose that you couldn't stay out there, but you had the feeling of wanting to get back in there and getting under that hot shower. Once you got up in the entry-way, sat down for a few minutes while the pots were being loaded, you'd start shaking uncontrollably; you weren't that cold, you weren't that uncomfortable but you just couldn't stop shaking." from *Groups Under Stress: Psychological Research in SeaLab II*

It became obvious that the wetsuit would not be adequate for extended dives in cold water at depth. At this point, divers began to experiment with other insulation systems. Experiments were done with non-compressible suits and *active heating systems.*

The Uniroyal Electrically heated suit. Note the electrical connections on the chest.

In 1965 the Uniroyal Corporation designed and tested an electrically heated suit for the SEALAB III project that was scheduled for placement off San Clemente island. Other companies produced similar suits, but all were plagued by hot spots, wire fatigue, bulk and weight. The idea was good, but the technology was not up to the task. Perhaps we'll see a return to this type of system at some date in the future, but at the time of this writing, no such system exists.

This Navy diver is fully geared up for SeaLab III.

Official U.S. Navy Photo by John Reaves.

This original waterproof zipper was quite different from those used today.

One of the most important spin-offs of the exploration of outer space was the development of the waterproof, pressure proof zipper. These zippers were made by B.F. Goodrich. Again, Bev Morgan was the innovator who first used a waterproof zipper in a dry suit in 1956. He made the suit from foam neoprene, with latex seals and an oral inflator. The suits were advertised in *Skindiver Magazine*.

Ingvar Elfstrom, a Swedish diver and inventor, developed the Unisuit with Peter Wide, a supervisor of diving for the Swedish Navy. Elfstrom, had been building and marketing regulators for many years through his company, Poseidon Industri AB, prior to the development of the Unisuit. The Unisuit was the first dry suit that included both a waterproof zipper, low pressure power inflator and exhaust valves. The suit was made from foam neoprene and the zipper ran though the crotch, from mid-back to mid-chest. Pile underwear by Helly Hansen provided the insulation beneath the suit.

The Unisuit quickly established itself as the most popular dry suit on the market. It was the standard by which all other dry suits were judged. Unisuits have been used around the world and were adopted by most navies during the 60's and early 70's. The suit is still popular today with many divers.

Meanwhile, in Norway, two divers collaborated on the development of the Viking suit. Stig Insulan, a former Swedish Navy diver and Jorn Stubdal, a commercial diver, worked on a vulcanized rubber dry suit, similar to those manufactured by Dunlop and Avon. Their teamwork resulted in many unique concepts for dry suits that are still in use today.

One of the most important contributions of Insulan and Stubdal was the refinement of the automatic exhaust valve for dry suits. In essence, they took the exhaust valve that had been in use on heavy gear helmets for over a century and redesigned it to mount on a dry suit. This development, in combination with the power inflator, gave the scuba equipped dry suit diver precise buoyancy control. Today, this valve is available on many different dry suits.

Insulan and Stubdal also developed a unique set of mannequins that were used to mold the Viking suits. The suits were assembled and pulled on the mannequins. The mannequins were then placed inside a giant vulcanizing chamber where the seams of the suit were sealed at a temperature of 250 degrees F.

The single most successful active heating system in diving has been the hot water suit. Originally, the hot water suit was developed by a French

photo by Bev Morgan

Bob and Bill Meistrell were co-owners of Dive N'Surf with Bev Morgan. In this 1956 photo, Bill (right) is wearing a suit with both an oral inflator and a CO2 inflator.

Ingvar Elfstrom, second from left, in an early Unisuit.

Dennis Osterlund, Aquasport.

diver named Dupre. The concept is very simple. The diver wears a loose fitting wetsuit that is supplied with hot water from the surface via a hose. The hot water flushes out through the zipper as well as the wrists, ankles, and neck of the suit. A boiler unit and a series of pumps on the surface keeps the suit continuously supplied with hot water. The effect is like diving in a bath tub of warm water. It is extremely comfortable and divers have made dives up to 16 hours in water temperatures in the low 40's wearing hot water suits. Although the hot water suit is a practical answer for the commercial diver using surface supplied (umbilical) diving equipment, it is impractical for a non-tethered, free swimming sport diver.

Westinghouse was very involved in diving during the 60's and had their own Man in the Sea program. Jerry O'Neill, an inventor and diver at Westinghouse, further developed the concept of the hot water suit and patented parts of the suit. They built several working units for the Smith

Stig Insulan, one of the co-inventors of the Viking suit, during the early days of diving.

Dick Long developed the hot water suit that made deep commercial diving possible.

Mountain Dam Project, the first commercial saturation diving job, but those first systems scalded the divers. At the time, they were unable to see the future applications for the gear and dropped further development.

With his insights from years of wetsuit design, Dick Long immediately saw the possibilities of the hot water suit. He continued development of the suit, and made it practical by adding tubes that would distribute the hot water to all the parts of the body.

But it wasn't enough just to develop the hot water suit, because without a reliable hot water source the suit wasn't usable. The heater required many different elements to make it a success. It required a pick-up pump that wouldn't clog if it sucked up a piece of debris, a burner that could operate on diesel fuel or other power source, a thermostat to keep the water at the right temperature, a control manifold to keep the diver from getting burned, and a pump that would deliver enough water through 1000 or more feet of hose.

During this same period, the offshore oil industry was starting to boom. There was an urgent need for divers to work deeper and longer than ever before. With the development of saturation diving it became possible to work efficiently at depths in excess of 300 feet for periods of up to a month. The saturation chamber complex permitted the divers to rest on the surface between dives, while still under pressure and living in the chambers. Each time the divers went to work they were lowered to the bottom in a diving bell where they locked out for dives of up to 4 hours. However, until the hot water suit was developed there was no efficient way to keep the diver warm and productive.

Through Dick Long's persistence, the hot water suit became an essential part of deep and cold water commercial diving as we know it today. By 1974, the hot water suit was firmly established in the commercial diving field.

Diving During the 1970's

During the 1970's there were very few new developments in thermal protection for divers. DUI was busily engaged in designing and building hot water systems for deeper and deeper diving. The Unisuit became popular with cold water divers around the world. New materials and insulators were being developed, but they had yet to be utilized by the diving industry.

One of the more popular dry suits that appeared during this period was the Supersuit manufactured by Jack O'Neill of Santa Cruz, California. The Supersuit had a trimmer fit than the Unisuit, with a zipper that ran across the diver's shoulder blades. This suit was made from neoprene rubber. Instead of a separate inflator and exhaust valve, the Supersuit used a power inflator from a buoyancy compensator mounted at the end of a corrugated hose. Since it was cheaper to manufacture, the Supersuit could be sold at prices well below the Unisuit. Many sport divers began to use the Supersuit in the temperate waters of California and at other locations in the U.S.

Jack O'Neill in a fully inflated Supersuit.

Variations of the Supersuit design began to appear on the market almost immediately. It was a simple matter for even a small manufacturer to buy the waterproof zippers and inflator mechanisms to build dry suits from neoprene. Many diving equipment manufacturers marketed suits similar to the Supersuit during this period.

One active heating product that never made it to market was a fuel burning diver heater developed in Japan. The system consisted of a small cannister with a metered orifice connected to a low pressure hose from the diver's regulator. The cannister was O-ring sealed. Inside the can, was a wick and a fuel compartment. After the can was filled with fuel and the wick was lit, the can was sealed. The outlet side allowed the heated air to escape. The can was designed to fit inside the diver's wetsuit. For a time, U.S. Divers considered distributing the product but ultimately rejected it.

Commercial diving operations during the 70's included the use of lockout submersibles, designed to carry saturation divers to work at depths in excess of 400 feet. The forward compartment of the subs carried a pilot and a life support operator at one atmosphere (surface pressure). The rear compartment carried a team of divers under pressure, capable of exiting the sub to do work. The subs were equipped with breathing gas supplies for the diver and a closed circuit diver heating system. The divers wore "tube suits" similar to those worn by the astronauts. Over the tube suits the divers would

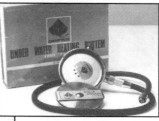

The Aqua Ardor diver heating system was developed by the Dampness Company in Japan.

Tube suits like this one were worn under dry suits by divers working out of lock-out submarines.

wear a variety of dry suit undergarments. Over the undergarments they wore a dry suit equipped with special inlet and outlet valves. The divers complained that it took over 45 minutes to dress into this equipment.

Hot water was pumped to the diver from the sub, circulated through the tube suit, and returned to the sub for reheating. In theory, it was a very productive system, but the subs were plagued by so many operational problems they are rarely used today. One of the major drawbacks was the limited weather conditions that were acceptable for launch and recovery of the subs themselves.

Viking began to actively import its suits into the United States during this period. Robert Shrout, a commercial diver in New York, was the first distributor of Viking suits in the United States. The first Viking suits in the U.S. were designed strictly for commercial diving and it wasn't until the early 80's that Viking manufactured suits for sport diving.

The 1980's: Dry Suit Use Becomes Widespread

By the early 1980's, many manufacturers were building a variety of dry suits from new materials, especially urethane laminates. The technology that was being used to manufacture buoyancy compensators was adopted by many companies to build dry suits.

Some of the biggest changes in the dry suit market were brought about by the introduction of new materials. TLS material, a tri-laminate of cloth and rubber, became available and was shown to be an excellent material for making dry suits. TLS was originally developed for use by NATO military forces in chemical warfare suits. It provides such an excellent liquid barrier that it makes an excellent material for dry suits. DUI introduced its patented CF200 material, a crushed neoprene with a heavy duty nylon coating that also quickly gained a following.

Better insulation materials also became available during this time. One of the most popular was Thinsulate®, manufactured by 3M and used in ski wear and other winter sports clothing. Max Lippett of the Naval Coastal Systems Lab was the first to appreciate the properties of Thinsulate® for underwater applications. Originally, type "M" Thinsulate® was used, but for underwater use the second generation that became known as Type "B" has proven best.

Thinsulate® proved to be an excellent choice for dry suit underwear because it provides warmth without bulk. Thinsulate® fibers are hydrophobic. i.e, they will not absorb water. In the event of a dry suit leak, Thinsulate® retains much of its insulating capacity.

Viking began distributing a relatively low cost, but effective underwear made from open cell foam. The material used was actually the same material used in the headliners from Volvo cars!

A new generation of synthetic pile fibers also became available that provided good insulation at a reasonable cost. The days of woolen underwear and inefficient sweat suits for dry suit diving were over.

With more reliable materials and better methods of construction, dry suit manufacturers turned their attention to making suits that were easier to use. Bob Stinton, DUI's chief engineer, came up with the idea for DUI's patented self-donning dry suit design in 1982. The idea was originally developed to allow a special forces diver to dress and undress himself during a mission. Simultaneously, Dick Long came up with the concept of using suspenders and a crotch strap on the suit to prevent the crotch of the suit from sagging. These combined features made it dramatically easier for a diver to walk, or even run, on dry land and to swim in the water.

Another active heating method that sport divers experimented with was the Heat Wave™ reusable diver heating pack. This system consists of a heavy duty plastic pouch filled with sodium acetate. The system is known as a "latent heat" system.

A trigger mechanism causes a chemical reaction known as a "phase change" inside the pouch that generates 130 degrees F heat for 30-45 minutes. This system generates 100 BTU's per pound, not enough heat to really keep a diver warm. In fact this localized heating method confuses the human body's physiological mechanism and can create a net overall heat loss. The skin senses temperature differential, not absolute temperature. This makes the diver subjectively feel warm. But, you may actually lose

Bob Stinton of Diving Unlimited developed the self donning suit for special operations divers.

more heat with this system than if the blood vessels under the skin are constricted as they would normally be in cold water.

By the mid 1980's there were many different types of dry suits from which to choose. Seatec, Viking, DUI, Harveys, OS Systems, SAS, Parkway, Henderson, KME, Avon, Typhoon, Poseidon, and Driflex were all building dry suits. By the end of the decade some of these manufacturers no longer made dry suits. New dry suits also became available from Nokia, Gates, U.S.I.A. and Mobby's.

Thermal Protection in the Year 2000

During the next ten years we expect to see new and even better materials on the market for dry suits and insulation. The dry suits we use today will undoubtedly become lighter weight and stronger.

With the advent of newer and better battery systems we may finally see a dry suit that uses an electrically heated undergarment. This could be an extremely thin garment that would dramatically cut the weight requirements for dry suit diving.

Other areas that are receiving attention at this time are the use of exotic gases for use inside the dry suit. By using a heavy gas, such as argon, the insulation capabilities of the underwear are improved and weight requirements are decreased. Whether argon is absorbed through the skin, creating problems with decompression, remains to be fully investigated.

Some divers are already using argon suit inflation systems on a regular basis with no apparent ill effects. Although there is considerable experience using argon in saturation diving and underwater welding, this system must still be viewed as experimental at this time.

Dry suit education has become a recognized specialty among the diver training agencies. NAUI, PADDI, and SSI all offer some type of dry suit diver specialty training. Many of the other training agencies will probably offer similar programs.

Chapter 2

Why Thermal Protection is Important

What is "cold" water?

One of the biggest problems in explaining a diver's need for thermal protection lies in defining the concept of "cold water". Every diver has a different range of temperatures that they find comfortable. There are many factors that influence a diver's subjective feelings of comfort in the water. These factors include the water temperature, the diver's size, the diver's percentage of body fat, the diver's activity level on any given dive, sleep before the dive, the type of thermal protection the diver is wearing, the duration of the dive, the number of preceding dives, and drug or alcohol use.

From an objective standpoint, we can say that a diver has begun to be affected by cold water when he or she exhibits certain measurable physiological and/or psychological signs. Some of the more obvious signs include, but are not limited to, shivering, discomfort, loss of manual dexterity, loss of reasoning ability, lapses in memory of events that occurred during the dive, and increased air consumption. These are all signs of hypothermia.

When these signs become so obvious as to be easily noticeable even to the diver's partner, it is probably long past the time when the diver should have left the water. Other effects are more subtle, but can be measured with the proper scientific instrumentation or tests.

Divers who regularly expose themselves to cold water become somewhat acclimated to the environment, showing a reduced physiological re-

Male and female divers have different reactions to, and perceptions of, cold water.

Even in tropical waters, it is a good idea to wear some type of thermal protection. For some divers a Lycra® skin might be enough, but you should wear whatever feels comfortable to you.

sponse. However, for a diver, it is impossible to totally eliminate the negative effects of cold water on your body.

Body Size and Structure are Important

One of the most important elements in determining how cold water affects a diver involves the surface area of the diver's body relative to their body mass. Given two divers of equal height, the diver who is more slender will usually chill faster. The more surface area the diver's body has, *relative to their body mass*, the faster that body will lose heat. Larger divers do not chill as quickly as smaller divers. Female divers usually have more surface area than males of similar height and will chill faster.

The old theory that females make better divers due to their extra layer of body fat is not true. Female divers will generally report subjective feelings of cold sooner than male divers.

Cold Water Effects

Divers who are cold use more air in the same period of time than divers who are warm. Scientific tests have shown that divers who are cold may increase their air consumption by up to 29% over divers who are kept warm in the same temperature water. If you want the longest possible bottom time from a scuba bottle, it is essential to ensure that you are wearing the right thermal protection for the water temperature in which you dive. Even in tropical waters, if you make multiple dives during the day, you will get longer bottom times if you wear a thin wetsuit rather than an ordinary Lycra® dive "skin".

The reason for this higher air consumption rate is very simple. The metabolism of a diver who is cold will increase as the body burns more calories in an attempt to maintain the proper internal temperature (core temperature). The diver's body will "burn" more fuel (nutrients) in an attempt to maintain the proper internal temperature. This process takes place inside the body without the diver being aware of it. For a diver who becomes chilled, there is a significant danger that the body will not be able to take in enough oxygen to meet both the demands of exercise and the increased metabolism to maintain the internal temperature. Without sufficient oxygen

Your bottom times will be longer in cold water if your are wearing the right thermal protection.

in your body you will feel fatigued. If the body is too cold, normal metabolic processes cannot take place.

Although you might not subjectively feel cold, after a day of diving in cold water, most divers will feel exhausted. The source of this fatigue is due to the energy requirements of diving in cold water. This "unearned fatigue" results when your cold body is unable to use fuel to replenish the energy in your muscles. If you have ever been diving in the tropics, compare how you felt after a day of diving in warm water to what you felt like after a day of similar activity in cold water. The difference is startling.

One of the ways that your body will attempt to control heat loss is through vasoconstriction. Vasoconstriction occurs when the body shuts down the circulation to the skin and extremities. If the water is cold enough, and the diver is not properly protected, the skin temperature will actually drop to a level close or equal to the surrounding water temperature.

Aside from the direct effect of cold water against the skin, there are other ways that divers lose body heat when diving in cold water. No matter what type of suit you are wearing, if you are using scuba you will lose body heat each time you exhale through your regulator. Three factors contribute to this situation. First, the air in the scuba tank is chilled to the surrounding water temperature in a very few minutes. You can confirm this by checking your submersible pressure gauge shortly after you enter the water. When the water temperature is colder than the air temperature topside, your tank pressure will drop due to the decreased temperature.

As you inhale through the second stage of your regulator, the air supplied by the first stage experiences a pressure drop. This pressure drop causes another decrease in the air temperature. You can see a similar effect by opening the valve on a bare scuba tank topside. As the air blasts out of

Respiratory heat loss in cold water is considerable. Every time you exhale underwater you lose body heat.

the tank, the tank will cool rapidly and condensation will form on the tank and valve.

The cold air you inhale from your regulator is warmed to your body temperature as it enters your body. If the water temperature is 50 degrees F and the internal body temperature is 98.6 degrees F, the temperature difference is 48.6 degrees. Each time you exhale a substantial amount of heat is lost from your body. This problem is compounded by the fact that scuba air is dry while your lungs are wet. Not only does this exhaled breath carry heat, it also carries moisture . The percentage of metabolic heat lost through breathing can exceed 20% depending upon your depth, lung volume, and exercise rate.

Heat and body fluids are also lost through urination. Divers wearing wetsuits commonly urinate in their suits in response to cold water exposure. This is caused by increased blood circulating through the kidneys as a result of vasoconstriction. As more blood volume is passed through the kidneys, more urine is produced. Each time that you urinate underwater, both heat and fluid are lost. This loss of body fluids can cause decompression problems and may contribute to bubble formation leading to decompression sickness.

Your body "knows" that you can live without your hands or feet, but your head and internal organs are essential to survival. Conversely, the brain and internal organs must be continuously supplied with heat, fuel, and oxygen by the blood. Unfortunately, since the head also has such a large surface area, it contributes to a significant loss of body heat. This makes it very important to have adequate thermal protection for your head in cold water. Estimates of the percentage of body heat lost through an unprotected head run as high as 50%.

For scuba divers, there is a real trade-off between adequate thermal protection for your hands and manual dexterity. The more insulation you wear on your hands, the less able you will be to operate equipment underwater. The loss in grip strength from a five fingered neoprene glove alone has been measured at 22%. Without proper warmth, nutrients, and oxygen, the muscles of the hands will not function properly.

Minimal hand insulation, such as thin gloves, will permit greater manual dexterity initially, but only until your hands become too cold to be useful. Divers equipped with active heating systems, such as hot water suits, don't suffer cold hands. However, the best passive insulation systems for scuba divers are not adequate for anything other than a relatively short exposure at water temperatures below 35 degrees F. *(See Chapter 7 for information on dry glove systems.)*

Memory is another area that seems to be affected by cold water exposures and lower body temperature. Divers who are affected by cold water may have trouble concentrating on simple tasks and multiple tasks may be impossible. In water temperatures below 50 degrees F, a diver's performance capability of complex tasks may decrease by as much as 20% or more. Similarly, divers who became chilled during a dive may not remember what they were supposed to achieve underwater, or the details of the dive after it is over.

Decompression sickness (bends) is another problem that can be compounded by exposure to cold water. A diver's blood will thicken due to the loss of body fluids by urination and breathing. This loss of fluids results in poor blood circulation. Reduced blood circulation to your extremities when you are cold in the water is just one of the factors that will make it more likely that you may suffer from the bends. Our goal is to keep the diver in *thermal equilibrium.*

While obviously not every diver who becomes chilled will suffer from de-

Divers who become chilled may be more susceptible to decompression sickness.

Proper hand protection is very important in cold water.

courtesy Nokia Safety

compression sickness, several recent studies indicate that there is a link between these two conditions. Scientists at the Naval Medical Research Institute and the Defense and Civil Institute of Environmental Medicine conducted a statistical analysis of experimental decompression dives. They compared test dive data from chamber experiments where 727 dives were made "wet", while 797 dives were made dry. The risk of decompression sickness increased by almost 30% during the dives where the divers were cold and wet.

Other cold water experiments have been conducted with the Doppler flow meter, a device that scientists use to detect nitrogen bubbles in diver's bodies. In tests where the arms and legs were chilled, but the diver's core temperatures remained stable, Doppler detectable bubbles were found in the diver's bodies.

The end result of exposing a diver to cold water without proper thermal protection is the increased risk of a diving accident. This probably occurs long before hypothermia sets in. Considering all of the possible combined negative factors, i.e., increased air consumption, increased fatigue, a loss of manual dexterity, and impaired mental capacity, it is easy to see why a diver who is chilled is a good candidate for a diving accident. Any time hypothermia becomes apparent the dive should be terminated.

The ultimate result of body heat loss is hypothermia, a condition where the diver's body core temperature drops. When your core temperature drops to approximately 97 degrees you will begin to shiver. If this condition persists, or your core temperature drops even fractionally lower, you will shiver uncontrollably. At a core temperature of 95 degrees F you will reach the point where clear thought becomes difficult. For most people, any drop in body temperature below this is considered intolerable. By the time your core drops to 93 degrees F you will be suffering from hallucinations. At this core temperature, up to 50% of all divers may die. Below 84 degrees F, unconsciousness is a certainty and at 81 degrees death results from heart stoppage (ventricular fibrillation).

Predicting Individual Needs for Underwater Thermal Protection

It is impossible to predict the insulation requirements for each individual diver in cold water. Two divers who are the exact same size may have very different metabolic characteristics. Their bodies produce heat and react to cold in different ways. Although we can make some general predictions regarding a diver's individual needs, it will be up to you to determine what feels best in a particular situation.

The Thermal Guidelines for divers were first developed by DUI and Dick Long in 1986. They were the first set of predictive tables to help determine the diver's thermal needs based upon multi dive exposures. The tables we have included in the appendix are the most recent version of the guidelines. They have been continuously refined since first being developed *(see Appendix A)*.

If we examine the relative efficiency of wetsuits compared to dry suits, we find that wetsuits become less acceptable when you make multiple dives in a single day. Part of the problem with the wetsuit is that as you exit the water, the water inside the suit that was warmed by your body drains out. On each subsequent dive, a new quantity of water must be warmed up.

Another problem that most people overlook is that as a wetsuit ages, it becomes less efficient over time. The closed cell neoprene material used to make the suit breaks down when exposed to pressure. In addition, if salt water drys in the suit, salt crystals can actually cut the individual cells, ruining their insulating capabilities. For this reason, active diving scientists replace their wetsuits every 2 to 3 years, even if the suit "looks okay".

Table 1 gives a rough comparison of wetsuits to dry suits. This table does not take into account body size, individual physiological differences, or the diver's activity level. It is only meant as a general comparison and a point of reference to start from when you evaluate what thermal protection you should choose.

Table 1:
Efficiency and Reliability of
Wetsuits vs. Dry Suits
During a 3 Dive Day

Water Temperature	WETSUITS			DRY SUITS		
	1st Dive	2nd Dive	3rd Dive	1st Dive	2nd Dive	3rd Dive
70⁰ F	100%	100%	100%	100%	100%	100%
60⁰ F	100%	90%	80%	100%	100%	100%
50⁰ F	80%	70%	50%	100%	100%	100%
40⁰ F	50%	25%	*	100%	85%	75%
32⁰ F	*	*	*	100%	75%	55%

Not recommended unless involved in a life saving rescue.
**Table based upon 30 minute dives at a depth of 50 feet, with a one hour surface interval between dives.*

To fully understand what thermal protection you should wear, based upon your body size and activity level, you first need to have an understanding of insulation. Chapter 6 provides a complete explanation of insulation.

Chapter 3

Contaminated Water Diving: When Staying Dry is Essential

What is contaminated water?

One of the more critical applications for dry suits is in contaminated water diving. We define contaminated water as any underwater environment that contains biological, chemical, or nuclear pollution that may be harmful to the diver. Harmful pollutants are those that will injure or kill the diver when taken into the body either directly through the skin, through breathing, or through accidental swallowing. The purpose of the dry suit is to keep the contaminants completely away from the diver's body.

Contaminated water diving is not for the amateur. It should only be undertaken by highly trained professional divers who have a specific reason for entering a polluted water environment. The risks involved in contaminated water diving are extremely high. Divers who were not properly prepared for this type of diving have died in contaminated water environments.

Contaminated water diving operations are not for the amateur diver. Commercial diver Jerry Clouser is also director of the Santa Barbara City College Marine Technology Program.

33

Who dives in contaminated water?

The need to dive in contaminated water environments varies from mission to mission. Water quality biologists may need to dive in contaminated water to take biological or chemical samples, or to make observations. Law enforcement divers regularly dive in polluted water to recover evidence, make rescues, or save lives. Fire fighters may be required to fight fires under piers where burning pilings release creosote or other chemicals. Fire fighters are also frequently called upon to deal with toxic spills. Military divers may be required to deal with biological or chemical warfare agents. Commercial divers must frequently dive in polluted harbors or other waterways to do their work. Some commercial divers also regularly work inside nuclear reactors.

Professionals who deal with hazardous materials on a regular basis have developed classifications for both the hazards and the level of protection required to deal with specific hazards. Exposure to certain biological or short term effects, such as causing diarrhea, nausea, or chemical burns. Other chemicals such as cancer causing agents, or radioactive materials, may have long term chronic effects. Certain other chemicals or biological materials may cause death after very short exposures.

> ## To dive in contaminated water requires, at a minimum, a dive team and support personnel with the following assignments:
>
> - Primary diver
> - Standby diver
> - Primary tender
> - Standby tender
> - Dive control system operator
> - Diving supervisor
> - Preliminary decontamination wash down team *(2 people)*
> - Definitive decontamination wash down team *(2 people)*
> - Back-up decontamination team *(2 people)*
> - Medical support personnel
> - Haz-mat *(hazardous materials)* supervisor
> - Incident command supervisor

Determining what equipment the diver should wear for a particular hazard requires the dive team to evaluate the effects of that hazard. Diving in contaminated water requires a coordinated team of highly trained divers and support people. It is not an activity that can be conducted by a single diver.

Depending upon the scope of the incident and the resources available, more support personnel may be involved.

Full face masks should be used for contaminated water operations only where there is no danger of permanent disability or death from contact with the contaminants involved.

Basic Equipment Decisions for Contaminated Water Diving

On dry land, unless you are dealing with a toxic substance that creates fumes or penetrates the skin easily, haz-mat personnel may only be equipped with little more than a "splash suit" and a respirator. Topside, this is considered "Level C" protection by haz-mat personnel. If you add a self contained breathing apparatus to the basic splash suit, then you have graduated to "Level B" protection. Incidents that demand complete encapsulation of topside personnel are said to demand "Level A" protection.

Underwater, however, where toxic substances are dispersed by the water, the contaminant may be suspended in solution and completely surround the diver. For this reason, a dry suit with attached boots, hood, and gloves is always required when diving in polluted water. The only other equipment variable that usually remains to be decided is whether to use scuba or surface supplied air, and whether to use a full face mask or a helmet.

Scuba operations in contaminated water are typically conducted with full face masks. With this type of equipment there is always the risk that the mask will come loose and leak. Communications with full face masks usually do not match the quality of those possible with a dry helmet. For these reasons, scuba operations in contaminated water with full face masks should be limited to those situations that present hazards that do not exceed short term illness or injury.

Full face mask scuba equipment is not recommended for most contaminated water diving operations for several reasons. Most critical is the fact that if you run out of air during a scuba operation there is a very serious risk of exposure to contaminants if you remove your mask to share air or breathe once you break the surface. Since most contaminated water diving operations tend to take place in environments with limited visibility, there is also a very real chance of entanglement.

Any contaminated water diving operation that presents the risks of chronic disability, carcinogens, or death should only be conducted with a dry suit that mates directly to a full coverage helmet, such as the SuperLite-

17®. This equipment is designed to be used in the surface supplied mode, the preferred method for all contaminated water diving operations. Surface supplied diving equipment has several major advantages over scuba for this type of work. The advantages include an unlimited air supply, hard wire communications, back-up breathing systems, topside depth monitoring, and a direct link to the surface.

The minimum diving equipment required for a surface supplied dive in biologically contaminated water includes a topside air supply with backup, an air supply manifold for controlling the air supply to the diver, a hard wire communications system, a diver's umbilical, a diver's full face mask or helmet, bail-out bottle, vulcanized rubber dry suit, and mating dry gloves. The standby diver must be equally equipped with the same mask or helmet, bail-out bottle, suit, and gloves.

Dry Suit Essentials for Contaminated Water Diving

Many tests have been conducted on dry suits and diving helmets for use in contaminated water diving operations. In regards to diving in biologically polluted water, the type of dry suits recommended by the Environmental Protection Agency (EPA) and the National Oceanographic and Atmospheric Administration (NOAA) are those made from vulcanized rubber.

Vulcanized rubber dry suits provide a very reliable level of protection in biologically contaminated water. They are especially easy to decontaminate due to their slick outer surface. After proper decontamination and once they have dried, there is very little chance that bacteria or other organisms will continue to grow on this material. In contrast to this, suits with an exterior nylon coating are very difficult to decontaminate properly. In scientific tests, high levels of bacteria have continued to grow on the surface of nylon coated suits even after they have been decontaminated.

Any dry suit that is used for contaminated water diving should be equipped with hard sole, attached boots. Latex socks are not acceptable for contaminated water diving because the risk of puncture, even with protective neoprene booties over them, is unacceptably high.

Divers with thin faces may have difficulty getting a proper seal between the full face mask and a latex hood. If this happens, the mask may inflate the hood making it very uncomfortable. Before you use this equipment in open water be sure to test it to see if this is a problem for you. If it is, you should have your dry suit dealer install the smallest hood available and it will probably solve the situation.

Viking offers a special patented hood especially for contaminated water diving operations. The Turbo hood has two layers; an inner latex layer and an outer layer of the same material as the suit. Before you purchase this type of hood you should test dive it to see if it works well for you. Due to the strength of the suit material, this can be a difficult hood for some divers to remove. In addition, the hood inflation problem mentioned with the latex hood can occur with the turbo hood as well.

Dry gloves are another essential piece of equipment for dry suit diving. Dry gloves, or mittens, are part of a system that consists of several parts. These parts include:

a) A set of inner cuff rings (one for each sleeve)
b) A set of outer cuff rings (one for each sleeve)
c) A set of dry gloves or mittens
d) Liners for gloves or mittens

This dry suit is equipped with a special mating yoke for the SuperLite-17® helmet.

The patented Viking Turbo hood is actually a double hood.

If you are diving with a full face mask the suit must be equipped with an attached latex hood. The hood is glued directly to the body of the suit so that no part of your neck or face is exposed. The full face mask must mate directly to the hood with no gaps. There must be no way for water to get past the face seal and into the mask. This type of hood must be worn with a liner that provides both insulation and an air volume for equalization. The pressure inside the hood must be equalized to prevent ear squeeze, but also must be vented upon ascent.

If you are diving with a full coverage helmet, such as a SuperLite-17® or a Desco, your suit must be equipped with a special yoke so that the helmet will mate directly to the suit. The yoke eliminates the gap that would exist at the neck if a conventional neck dam was used with the helmet.

The minimum suit material weight for contaminated water diving is 1000 grams per square meter. Vulcanized rubber dry suits that are lighter than this, such as those used for sport diving, are not robust enough for contaminated water diving operations.

It must be kept in mind that there is no one dry suit material that will be compatible with all chemicals under all conditions. Every chemical hazard varies with the nature of the chemical, the concentration of the chemical(s), time of exposure, and temperature. The diver must not dive unless he or she knows exactly what hazards are present, their effect on the body and equipment, and what decontamination procedures must be followed. However, divers should keep in mind that even a mild chemical exposure can alter equipment in ways that are not easily detectable. These exposures can cause the equipment to fail unexpectedly in chemical environments that otherwise might be considered acceptable.

Most commercially available dry suits are made from a combination of synthetic and natural rubber that is easily assembled and vulcanized. However, a dry suit can be made from other combinations of materials that will give an equally smooth outer surface. The new material that the U.S. Navy is currently investigating for diving in chemically polluted water is a combination of viton/chlorobutyl. This material looks promising, but it is difficult to produce a reliable seam when incorporated in a diving suit. Hypalon is another material that has been investigated, but no off-the-shelf suits are available in this material at the time of this writing.

Various dry suit materials and diving equipment were tested by the Texas Research Institute for the Naval Surface Weapons Center. They tested the equipment in concentrated chemicals and in reduced chemical concentrations. They also conducted burst tests on diving hoses after exposing them to a variety of chemicals.

The most important tests conducted for the Navy were the permeation of the suit material by the various chemicals. Permeation is the transfer of a chemical through a material at the molecular level. Certain chemicals will actually "wick" through the material without causing visible damage to the material, but can still harm the diver. The tests in Table 2 reflect the results with the Viking suit as it was manufactured in 1983. Since manufacturing processes and materials are changed by manufacturers without notice, these results are only presented for informational purposes. They may not accurately represent the results that would be obtained with a current model of Viking suit. (For further information on equipment chemical compatibility, and a complete explanation of contaminated water diving procedures see *Diving in High Risk Environments* by Steve Barsky.)

Table 2:
Permeation Results Concentrated Chemical Exposure (Standard: ASTM-F-739)
Test Results:
Viking Heavy Duty Suit, 1983 SpecificationsTests Conducted by Texas Research Institute for Naval Surface Weapons Center

Chemical	Result	Breakthrough Time
Hydrochloric Acid	Passed	
Formaldehyde	Failed	20 Hours
Phenol	Passed	
Ethyl Amine	Failed	20 Hours
Acrylonitrile	Failed	3 Hours
Ethylene Glycol	Passed	
JP-4 Jet Fuel		
Super Tropical Bleach	Passed	
DS-2	Passed	
AFFF	Failed	20 Hours
Oregano Tin Paint	Passed	
Methyl Ethyl Ketone (10%)	Failed	1/2 Hour
Sulfuric Acid (10%)	Failed	20 Hours
Phenol *	Passed	
Hexane *	Failed	1/2 Hour
Diethyl Ether	Failed	1/2 Hour
Gasoline	Failed	1/2 Hour

* Concentrated exposure for 5 minutes followed by exposure to saturated solution.

Warning: Test results apply to new, unused materials. Equipment that has been exposed to other chemicals may perform differently.
Warning: Test results presented here are for information purposes only. No predictions or recommendations for exposures are made by the authors.

Due to the stringent requirements for this type of diving, at a minimum, one third of all equipment used in contaminated water diving should be scheduled for replacement on an annual basis. Depending upon the chemicals involved, certain items of diving equipment may need to be replaced after a single exposure.

Basic Contaminated Water Diving Procedures

To fully understand contaminated water diving we can best illustrate the procedures involved through an imagined hazardous materials incident. The procedures and methods presented here do not begin to cover all of the details, preparations, and techniques that are involved in safely handling a hazardous materials incident. In addition, as technology changes, some of these procedures will undoubtedly be improved. We only present this example to give the reader an idea of the complexity of a hazardous materials incident where divers are involved.

Our hypothetical scenario involves a truck carrying toxic waste that has gone off a bridge into a shallow lake. The driver is trapped inside the cab underwater. One side of the truck can be seen from the bridge

The dive team that is dispatched to respond to the incident is part of the fire department's hazardous materials team. They have all of the proper equipment for decontamination. The local police department has also been dispatched to provide control of the area.

At the site, the fire department uses tape to cordon off the area. The lake itself is considered to be the center of the "hot zone", the center of the contaminated site. The incident command post is set up on the upwind side of the bridge. In the event the truck starts to leak and release hazardous fumes, the public safety personnel should not be downwind of the fumes.

From the chemical warning labels on the side of the truck the divers can determine who owns the vehicle. They contact the owner of the vehicle and are able to get information on what chemicals the truck is carrying. They determine that their diving gear is compatible with the chemicals in the truck, and that there will be no reaction between these chemicals that will produce other more dangerous chemicals.

The decontamination equipment is set up so that the divers can be properly washed down after the dive. There is the proper equipment on hand to collect all of the water and chemicals used in the washdown process.

The diver is dressed into a vulcanized rubber dry suit with a mating helmet. Surface supplied equipment is chosen due to the fact that one of the chemicals is a carcinogen.

The tenders who will handle the diver's hose are also dressed into the appropriate haz-mat gear for topside protection. Since they will be directly handling the wet hose they will need a very high level of protection.

Once the diver is dressed in, he enters a small portable water tank filled with clean water. The dive team supervisor carefully observes the diver to make sure there are no leaks in the diver's suit or helmet that would allow dangerous chemicals to enter.

After it has been determined that the diver's equipment is working properly he is led to the side of the bridge. The diver and tender pass from the support zone, where the diver was dressed, into the contamination reduction zone. To do so, they go through a cordoned off area where the decontamination will take place. Plastic tarps are spread on the ground to catch the chemicals and water used during the decontamination process.

Entry and exit from the water is always made at the same point, the access control point. Objectives for the dive will be to recover the driver of the truck and determine if there is any chemical leakage into the lake.

Decontamination of a diver after a dive in a simulated biologically contaminated environment.

The diver enters the water and removes the body of the driver. The driver's body is placed in a body bag and removed from the lake. The diver determines that none of the drums of chemicals appears to be leaking.

With his tasks completed, the diver exits the water. At the top of the ladder, the diver is given a preliminary wash with fresh water. He then is led to the decontamination area, more properly known as the contamination reduction corridor.

The diver is carefully washed down before any equipment is removed. This should take place in some type of portable pool where the waste water can be captured for removal.

The nature of the contamination will determine what decontamination solutions are used. In the case of biological contaminants, some of the more common solutions used include a variety of soaps. In the case of chemical hazards, the decontamination solution selected must be one that neutralizes the specific chemical(s).

After the diver's equipment is removed, it is bagged for a more complete breakdown and cleaning later. The diver then proceeds to a special trailer where he removes any remaining clothing and showers. After drying, the diver disposes of his towel in a special bin and proceeds to a second shower. The second towel is also discarded. The diver then dresses and is examined by medical personnel. Training is Required

Chapter 4

Types of Dry Suits

Today's dry suits are very different from the dry suits first used for sport diving. New materials make the modern dry suits lighter, tougher, and more resistant to abrasion. Used properly, dry suit valves provide incredibly precise buoyancy control. Waterproof zippers make the suits easy to don and remove. Improved construction techniques give many dry suits a longer useful life than most wetsuits. Advanced features offer more comfort and improved fit. With all of the features available in dry suits today, it's possible to construct a dry suit that will precisely fit your needs.

Features of Dry Suits

Buying a dry suit is a bit like buying a car; there are many options available. The price you pay for a dry suit will largely be determined by the material, its capabilities, and the number of options you select. Generally speaking, the more options on the suit, the more expensive it will be. However, these options can make a big difference in how much enjoyment you get out of your dry suit.

In this chapter we'll discuss the various features available in today's dry suits, with the exception of dry suit valves. Dry suit valves are a more specialized topic and will be covered separately in Chapter 5.

Dry Suit Zippers

The zippers used in dry suits are very similar to the zippers used in an astronaut's space suit. Dry suit zippers must be both waterproof and pressure proof.

Dry suit zippers are not built by any of the dry suit manufacturers. Instead, most dry suit manufacturers buy the hardware for their suits, such as zippers and valves, from a few suppliers. In many cases, the zippers used on competing dry suits are purchased from the same supplier, but manufactured to different specifications. There are three principal manufacturers of dry suit zippers; Dynat, Talon and YKK. All of these manufacturers make good quality zippers from similar materials and machinery.

The zipper teeth are made from bronze. They seal by compressing a rubber sealing surface between the inner teeth of the zipper. Every dry suit zipper includes three essential parts; the slider, the teeth, and the tape.

Dry suit zippers should be as rugged as possible. Stronger zippers last longer, but they are also more expensive. Selecting a dry suit zipper is a trade-off between durability and cost. Larger zippers may be a bit more durable, but they are also more difficult to close and more restrictive to your movement in the water. When you purchase a dry suit, compare zippers between different brands of suits. Check with other divers to see what they have found to be most reliable.

Dry suit zippers can not be repaired if the tape is torn or the teeth "split" behind the slider. This means that once your zipper goes bad, it must be replaced. This is an expensive process, partly because the zipper is costly, and partly because it takes a qualified dry suit repair person to replace a zipper. The most common zipper failure occurs when the tape tears between the teeth. Sliders can also fail.

The only zippers that can be repaired are the heavy duty zippers used on some suits designed for commercial diving. The zipper teeth on these suits are individually pinned. They can be replaced providing the base material of the zipper is still in good condition. These zippers are much more expensive than the regular zippers used on most sport diving suits.

Suspenders
(also known as "braces" in Great Britain)

Suspenders are one of the features that can help make the difference between a truly comfortable dry suit and one that is just tolerable. On some dry suits suspenders are an option, while on others they are included as standard.

Most dry suits are cut somewhat loose and baggy. This is a necessity to give you the room to get your arms, legs, and head into the suit because most dry suit materials don't stretch. The extra room also allows for changes in underwear thickness during different seasons. This also allows dry suits to tolerate changes in your personal body weight much better than wetsuits.

A dry suit zipper consists of the tape base, a set of teeth, and a slider.

Ankle straps are another feature that will help your suit to fit better.

Suspenders make your suit more comfortable to wear between dives and in the water. Dick Long gears up to dive at Santa Cruz Island.

Once the suit is on, the suit hangs from your shoulders. Without suspenders, a substantial amount of material will hang down in your crotch. This excess material makes it more difficult to swim, walk, or climb a ladder. The effect of this excess material is roughly equivalent to tying a rope around your thighs and trying to swim. It's possible to move, but you don't have the same range of motion. Divers who use suits without suspenders usually pull their suits up around their waist just before they enter the water.

Dry suits equipped with suspenders are much more comfortable to wear. You adjust the suspenders to pull the excess material snugly up into your crotch. This makes the dry suit fit and feel better. You will find you have greater freedom of movement while wearing a dry suit that comes with suspenders compared to a similar suit with no suspenders.

Another nice thing about suspenders is that they allow you to peel the top of your dry suit down between dives, without having the suit fall off. This makes it very comfortable to walk around on the deck of a boat or on the beach.

Ankle Straps

Ankle straps are another feature that will make your dry suit easier to use. Although they are not mandatory in a dry suit, ankle straps also help your suit to fit better. Ankle straps gather the dry suit material at your ankle and decrease the air volume in the suit.

This Tornado Pro-Am suit from Parkways has latex seals on the wrists and the neck. Photo courtesy of Parkways.

Trimming a latex neck seal is much easier when your buddy helps you.

Most dry suits today come with attached hard sole boots. One of the important safety aspects of ankle straps is that they help to keep your feet secure in your dry suit boots. Ankle straps also help reduce the volume of air in your dry suit boots when you are inverted.

In the rare event you lose control of your buoyancy and your dry suit boots fill with air, ankle straps will help prevent your feet from coming out of your boots. If your feet pop out of your boots, your fins will pop off, making it difficult to regain control. This situation must be avoided. Proper training and diving procedures should prevent this from happening, but if it does it becomes an emergency of the highest order.

Crotch Straps

Crotch straps usually come as standard equipment in dry suits that have a telescoping torso for self-donning. In a self-donning dry suit, the torso of the suit "telescopes" or extends to aid entry into the suit. Once the suit is zipped, the telescoping portion of the suit folds under and is held in place with a crotch strap. Underwater, the water pressure actually holds the suit in position.

Wrist and Neck Seals

There are two types of seal materials that are commonly used for dry suit wrist and neck seals. Latex is one popular material and neoprene is another. Each material has its own set of advantages and disadvantages. Latex seals are the most common dry suit seals in use today. Latex seals have good stretch and provide a very smooth fitting, comfortable seal. They create the least pressure on the diver's wrists and neck.

It is important to remember that all seals can restrict blood flow somewhat. At the neck, this means too tight a neck seal will mean less blood going to your head. Restricted blood flow also means restricted heat flow to the extremities.

Dry suit seals are supplied in a cone or "bell" shape. Since most dry suits are sold as stock suits, it is not possible for the manufacturer to know the neck size of the person who buys the suit. By supplying seals that are cone shaped each diver can trim the neck seal to the size they feel is most comfortable.

Many divers like latex seals because they are very quick to repair. A puncture in a latex seal can be fixed with patches similar to those used to repair inner tubes.

Latex material has better "memory" than solid or foam neoprene rubber. This means that a latex seal tends to return to the same diameter whenever it is removed from your neck. By contrast, a neoprene neck seal can be stretched to a new size and tends to get looser as the neoprene becomes permanently stretched.

New latex seals almost always need to be trimmed for use by the diver. Generally speaking, the circumference of a latex seal should be just a bit smaller than the circumference of your neck or wrist at the smallest part. The exact size will vary with the thickness of the seal material. The seal must be snug enough to be watertight, but not so tight as to interfere with circulation.

To trim a latex neck seal, it's a good idea to have your buddy help you. Have your buddy hold the seal at opposite ends so that the neck opening is pinched together. This will, in effect, create two "edges" to the seal. Your buddy should pull the two ends away from each other so that the latex is under a slight tension. You are actually cutting through two thicknesses of material at the same time.

Both "edges" of the seal must be parallel to each other. Use the sharpest, largest scissors you can find and trim the seal, 1/4 inch down at a time. Make the longest cut possible as you trim to avoid nicks or rough edges. Try the seal on when you are close to the circumference you want to achieve.

When you get close to the final cut, stop! Try the seal on and see how it fits. If it is snug, but not uncomfortable you may want to try it as it is for a day of diving. You can always trim additional material off later. Test the size of the neck seal with your chin up. This makes the muscles in your neck tighter and your neck bigger.

Be careful not to trim too much, because once you have gone too far it is impossible to reattach the latex. If this happens you will need to install an entirely new neck seal.

New neoprene neck seals should be stretched over a scuba tank if they need adjustment. Allow them to stand for 24 hours.

Latex seals are more easily punctured or torn than neoprene seals. You must be very careful with your fingernails, watch, or jewelry when handling latex seals. However, properly maintained latex seals should last anywhere from 9 months to 2 years depending upon the amount of diving you do, the care the seals receive, and the ozone level where you live.

Heavy duty latex wrist seals are available and many divers use them. Heavy duty seals are much more rugged than ordinary seals and are also easier to install. They are definitely recommended for the diver who is rough on his or her equipment. Removing heavy duty latex seals can be a bit more difficult than removing an ordinary latex seal.

Keep in mind that any wrist seal can and will leak a little bit of water from time to time, especially if you have prominent wrist tendons. In addition, if you do a lot of work with your hands or make unusual movements as you operate your equipment, this may cause some leakage, too.

Neoprene wrist and neck seals don't stretch as much as latex and some divers find them uncomfortable. Neoprene does not have the same memory as latex. When it is stretched it takes on a new size. Neoprene seals are normally stretched to fit the individual diver. They should never be trimmed.

Small people with slender necks may find neoprene seals difficult to use or uncomfortable. If a neoprene seal is a problem the diver should switch to a latex seal. Also if you experience any visual disturbances you should switch to a latex seal.

The major advantage to neoprene seals is that they are more rugged than latex seals. They last longer and are more difficult to tear. The disadvantage to neoprene seals is that when they do tear, it takes longer for the glue in a permanent repair to dry properly. It also takes more skill to attach a neoprene seal properly.

Ordinarily, neoprene neck seals may be ordered in different sizes, but they may still need to be stretched. To make a new neoprene neck seal larger, you can stretch the material overnight using a scuba tank or a 3 pound coffee can for the shape. After stretching, try the neck seal on to see how it fits. As with any neck seal, if it feels comfortable, dive it for a day before you make any further adjustments. A neck seal that is a little bit uncomfortable out of the water may feel just fine underwater.

If the seal is still not comfortable, it may be necessary to stretch it again. Never trim a neoprene neck seal! Neoprene seals have a nylon lining that limits the amount of stretch the material possesses. If you have a very large neck you may need to use a large diameter seal.

Over time, neoprene neck seals will become thinner as the cells in the neoprene stretch. This will change

These Harvey's suits all come with attached boots.

the fit of the neck seal, making it looser. This is one of the reasons why it is important not to stretch a neoprene neck seal too far.

Neoprene wrist seals may be either cone shaped or may be designed to fold under like a neoprene neck seal. Cone-shaped seals are easier to don.

Attached Boots

Most modern dry suits are manufactured with attached hard sole boots. There are several advantages to this arrangement. First, by combining the dry suit and boots together, your feet stay dry and warm. Since heat loss through the feet can be very high, this is a very important consideration. In certain situations, such as contaminated water diving this is essential.

Another important benefit of attached boots is that it eliminates the seals that would be necessary at the ankles. Most people cannot get a good seal on their ankles due to their tendons. On men, hair on the ankles can also interfere with the seal.

Another drawback to ankle seals is that they reduce thecirculation to the feet. Attached dry suit boots make a major difference in warmth.

Some older dry suits are equipped with latex socks. If you use this type of suit you should use a pair of ordinary wetsuit booties to protect the thin latex material. Like latex seals, the latex socks will need to be replaced periodically. Latex socks are also extremely slippery when wet, but it can be difficult to don wetsuit booties over them when the proper insulation is worn under them

A side benefit of attached hard sole boots is that as long as you remember your dry suit, you will never forget your boots!

Dry Suit Hoods

If the water is cold enough to wear a dry suit, you will almost certainly want to wear some type of hood. There are many types of hoods available and you should carefully evaluate which style best meets your diving needs.

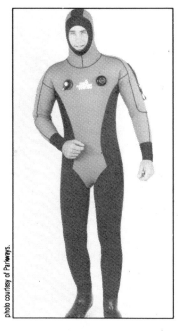

This Parkways suit has an attached neoprene hood.

A typical dry suit hood from foam neoprene material.

The simplest hood arrangement is to use a separate wetsuit hood. Wetsuit hoods are relatively inexpensive and require little maintenance. They are easy to don and remove and comfortable over a wide range of water temperatures.

Most ordinary wetsuit hoods come with a bib that allows you to tuck them under a wetsuit jacket. On most dry suits, however, there is no way to tuck the bib of a wetsuit hood under the neck seal without causing the suit to leak. One option found on some dry suits is a special "warm neck collar". This collar is mounted on the exterior of the dry suit, outside of the neck seal. The warm neck collar will allow you to tuck the wetsuit bib in between the body of the dry suit and the collar. This reduces the amount of cold water that comes up under the hood and adds quite a bit of extra warmth in colder waters.

If you already have a wetsuit hood with a bib, but your dry suit does not have a warm neck collar, you may want to remove the bib. This will help to keep the bib from floating up in your face. Use a large scissors to make a clean cut. Apply wetsuit cement to the ends of the stitching to prevent the seams from unraveling. However, you'll be more comfortable if you buy a hood designed to be used with a dry suit.

Some manufacturers also make special dry suit hoods that are cut off square at the collar. These are designed to seal on a neoprene neck seal.

If you use a wetsuit hood with your dry suit, you'll find that the most comfortable hoods are "vented". The vents are tiny holes in the hood that allow air that escapes from your mask or neck seal to drain out of the hood. Without vent holes the hood will fill with air, putting pressure on your mask. This makes diving very uncomfortable. Better vented hoods are equipped with a baffle system to help keep water out while allowing air to escape. These hoods must fit snugly to work properly.

Some dry suits are equipped with neoprene hoods attached directly to the suit. This arrangement is warmer than a separate wetsuit hood, but also makes the suit more difficult to don and remove. In addition, most divers find an attached neoprene hood is very bulky out of the water when pulled back. It is usually more convenient to have a separate neoprene hood.

A dry suit can be equipped with a hood that will keep your head dry, too. Two types of dry hoods are available. The first is a simple latex hood, made from exactly the same material as wrist seals and neck seals. This type of hood can be glued directly to the suit or can be attached with a neck ring. An inner liner must be worn for the latex hood to keep you warm. The second is a patented hood

Viking's dry hood is designed to be used with an inner liner.

developed for Viking by Jorn Stubdal and Stig Insulan. This hood is known as the turbo hood.

Viking's turbo hood is actually a double hood. It consists of an inner hood of latex and an outer hood made from the same vulcanized rubber Viking uses for their suits. The turbo hood was designed for use in demanding diving conditions, such as search and rescue or contaminated water. It was not designed for casual sport diving. One of the drawbacks to this type of hood is that on some divers, depending upon the shape of your head, it tends to fill with air. This may cause excessive buoyancy and neck strain.

Neither of the dry hoods will work properly if you have a beard. Beard hairs will break the seal allowing air to leak out and water to leak in. If you have a beard, an ordinary wetsuit hood may be your best option for use with your dry suit.

Knee Pads

Knee pads are standard equipment on most dry suits. They are absolutely essential for all divers, but particularly important for underwater photographers, lobster divers, and wreck divers.

Knee pads on foam neoprene suits can be a problem, however, since the cells of the foam material break down under the knee pad. The material becomes spongy and impossible to keep dry.

Most dry suit knee pads are made from the same material as the base material of the dry suit itself, although some are heavier. Keep in mind that all knee pads restrict movement to a certain degree and make it more difficult to swim.

Photo courtesy Scubapro.

These Scubapro dry suits come with generous knee pads.

Instructional Manual

Although this book is the most comprehensive dry suit diving reference available, we strongly recommend you select a dry suit that comes with a good user manual. Since each dry suit is different, and features change regularly, you need a good user manual. You'll want to read the manual for your particular suit to ensure that you understand any features or techniques that are unique to your dry suit.

Ease of Repair

Most dry suits today are relatively easy to repair. You can do most of the normal repairs yourself. We will show you the more common techniques in Chapter 12. We will also explain some tricks that you can use for emergency field repairs to keep you in the water.

Certain dry suit repairs are more complicated. For example, zipper replacement should only be done by an authorized repair facility.

Certain types of suits are quicker to repair than others. For example, TLS suits and vulcanized rubber suits dry more quickly than foam neoprene suits allowing you to repair them sooner.

Guarantee

Some dry suit guarantees are only for one year, while other manufacturers offer extended warranties. Ask to see the manufacturer's written warranty before you buy any dry suit so you will understand exactly what you are getting for your money. Bear in mind that you will always pay for repair work, one way or the other.

Most diving equipment manufacturers will stand behind their products quite well. However, be sure to read the manufacturer's warranty before you purchase your suit. Read it carefully so you understand exactly what is covered and what is not.

Reputation of the Manufacturer

One of the best ways to ensure that you are getting a good dry suit is to deal with a reputable manufacturer. Generally speaking, most of the people who manufacture dry suits are specialists. Dry suit manufacturing is usually their principal business. Very few full line manufacturers are in the dry suit game.

Check to see how long the manufacturer has been in business. Companies that produce poor products or treat customers shabbily usually don't last too long.

Reliability

Dry suit manufacturing techniques have been perfected to a very high level. The question of reliability is not the issue it was in the past.

The lifespan of a dry suit is dependent on many factors including the type of suit material and adhesives, use of the suit, seam construction, maintenance, and storage. Improper storage and poor maintenance can destroy a suit sooner than heavy use.

Dry suits definitely require more maintenance that wetsuits. However, with proper care, most dry suits will last much longer than a wet suit. You'll also get more diving for your dollar since you'll be able to make more dive in colder waters more comfortably.

Custom Vs. Stock Sizing

A dry suit need not fit you perfectly. Dry suits are designed to fit somewhat loosely, to accommodate a range of underwear combinations. If you have an "average" body, you probably can wear a stock dry suit. However if you are unusually thin, tall, short, or stocky, you may want a custom dry suit.

The advantage of a custom dry suit is that it can be tailored more closely to your body shape. A suit that is made for you will have a minimal internal volume and hold less air. For this reason, a custom suit will let you dive with considerably less weight than a stock dry suit. In addition, a custom suit will have less excess material to create drag.

Almost all dry suits can be ordered in custom sizes. However, some can be tailored from scratch where others (such as vulcanized rubber suits) can only be modified after the basic suit is assembled.

Prices

The initial investment for a dry suit and underwear will be more expensive than for a wetsuit. Yet in the long run, if you dive often, a dry suit is more economical than a wetsuit. This is particularly true if you participate in multi-day boat diving trips in cold water. Your cost per dive will be lower overall.

Boat diving in a wetsuit in cold water can be very fatiguing. With each successive dive, you lose body heat. It is not uncommon to see wetsuit divers stop diving for the day after the second or third dive in moderately cool water. In contrast, a dry suit diver remains comfortable on dive after dive, and is able to make as many dives as they like (within no-decompression limits). This makes each individual dive less expensive. Here's an example:

Suppose you pay $60.00 to go out on a single day boat trip. Let's suppose that the water temperature is 52 degrees F. If you wear a wetsuit and "freeze out" after two dives, your cost per dive is $30.00.

Compare this to using a dry suit. If you make just one more dive, your cost per dive drops to only $20.00. If you can make 4 dives that day, and this is entirely possible on many dive boats, your cost drops to $15.00 per dive. You'll probably not only make more dives per day, but your bottom time on individual dives will undoubtedly be longer. In addition, you'll make each additional dive in comfort, rather than shivering before, during, and after each subsequent dive. If you credited the cost of these "extra dives" against the cost of your dry suit, you would find they pay for the dry suit in a short time.

Types of Dry Suit Material

There are numerous types of dry suit material commonly available. As new fabrics are developed, we will certainly see additional new materials put to use. Any material that is waterproof and can be adequately joined together, or "seamed" could conceivably be used to create a dry suit.

The most common materials used for dry suits at this time are foam neoprene, crushed neoprene, urethane coated fabrics, tri-laminate fabric, Gore-tex®, and vulcanized rubber. Each material has its own set of characteristics that will affect the performance of the dry suit and the way it can be used.

SAS makes the Comfort Suit, a popular foam neoprene dry suit.

Foam Neoprene Dry Suits

There are numerous types of foam neoprene dry suits. Many are made by local wetsuit shops that specialize in custom dry suits from foam neoprene. These suits are among the least expensive of all types of dry suits.

Foam neoprene dry suits are assembled from sheets of neoprene rubber, the same material used to make wetsuits. The rubber is cut to the pattern of the panels of the suit. The material is glued together using wetsuit cement. Since wetsuit material is used, any color of neoprene material used for a wetsuit can also be used for a dry suit.

Each seam of the suit is stitched on a sewing machine with heavy duty thread. Normally, a "blind" stitch, that doesn't penetrate through the suit, is employed. To help ensure the integrity of the seams, some manufacturers coat the seams and use special sealing techniques.

Foam neoprene dry suits are usually shoulder entry suits, with a zipper running across the diver's back horizontally between his shoulder blades. Some of the lower priced suits use inflators similar to those used on buoyancy compensators, with a corrugated hose and mouthpiece.

One of the advantages of this type of system is that air can also be added to the suit orally. The disadvantage to this system is that when you push the exhaust button on the power inflator, to let air out of the suit, water will normally enter the mouthpiece and run into the suit.

Some foam neoprene dry suits are equipped with attached boots, while others are supplied with ankle seals instead. Suits that are designed this way must be used with wetsuit booties. These suits cost less, but offer less thermal protection.

Neck seals, on most foam neoprene suits are made from thin, 1/8 inch thick foam neoprene, while the wrist seals are 1/4 inch thick. Although latex seals can be attached to a foam neoprene suit, this is not a standard procedure for the majority of manufacturers.

Crushed neoprene dry suits, like this CF200 suit by DUI, are very popular with wreck divers.

Most foam neoprene suits are tailored to fit the body rather closely. In fact, in many cases, divers do not use much additional insulation underneath them. They merely rely on the inherent insulation of the neoprene itself and the layer of air trapped inside it. This arrangement will work in moderate waters and shallow depths, but will not be satisfactory for colder or deeper waters. In northern California, where scuba may not be used for abalone diving, foam neoprene dry suits are popular with many divers.

In situations where a foam neoprene dry suit leaks, you still have the benefit of the insulation of the neoprene material. Foam neoprene dry suits are also the only type of dry suit that are inherently buoyant. With a snug fitting foam neoprene suit, with little or no additional insulation, even if the suit floods completely you won't experience much of a change in buoyancy. Loose fitting foam neoprene suits, such as a Unisuit, will experience a greater buoyancy change if the suit no longer holds air.

All foam neoprene suits suffer from a loss of buoyancy and insulation at depth, just as a wetsuit does. This drawback should be considered by any serious diver before purchasing a suit of this type.

Over time, the buoyancy and insulation capabilities of a foam neoprene dry suit will decrease as the cells of the suit break down. Each time you dive, a certain number of cells collapse due to the increased pressure underwater. If you bump into a solid object with any force while wearing the suit you will also destroy a certain number of cells. Just the action of swimming, bending, and working with your arms will also break down the neoprene cells, especially in high wear areas like the knees, shoulders, and elbows.

Once the cells of the suit begin to break down it is very difficult to keep a neoprene dry suit dry. They will begin to weep water into the suit. The only way to repair a suit in this condition is to actually cut out and remove the damaged section of the suit.

Punctures in neoprene dry suits are difficult to locate and repair. Any puncture introduces water into the cellular material of the suit. Repairs to a foam neoprene suit can only be performed when the suit is completely dry. This can take many hours. In reality, water in the cells rarely ever dries completely.

The life expectancy of a neoprene dry suit will vary between 200 and 300 dives, depending upon your individual style of diving and the care you give your suit. To a certain extent, the material itself will stiffen, age and deteriorate. Smog and ozone are particularly detrimental to all types of diving gear, especially neoprene.

Foam neoprene dry suits are made by KME, Harvey's, Poseidon, DUI, and Parkway, as well as many local manufacturers, such as Monterey Bay Wetsuits in California.

Crushed Neoprene Dry Suits

Crushed neoprene material is a very tough, yet flexible material. It is an excellent material to use to make a dry suit.

Crushed neoprene starts out as a thick sheet of foam neoprene rubber. An extremely heavy duty nylon is bonded to the neoprene. The material is then pressurized so that all of the cells of the neoprene collapse. The resulting material is very thin, has a great deal of stretch, and is extremely rugged. The nylon used on the exterior of crushed neoprene material is among the most abrasion resistant of all dry suit materials.

The U.S. Navy selected crushed neoprene for their dry suit system. They call their combination of dry suit and underwear the "Passive Diver Thermal Protection System" (PDTPS).

Dry suits made from crushed neoprene can be tailored from start to finish. This helps give the suit an outstanding fit. Due to the tremendous stretch of crushed neoprene, the suit can be tailored for a very snug fit. The material is very difficult to assemble because it is so thin, but once assembled a very supple suit results.

When a dry suit is assembled from crushed neoprene the material is glued together, then stitched with a blind stitch. The nylon is then removed 1/4 inch either side of the internal seams and coated with an elastomeric material. This assures watertight integrity. This process is patented. Crushed neoprene dry suits are normally supplied with foam neoprene seals. However, these suits are also available with latex seals.

Properly fitted, crushed neoprene dry suits typically have a very low internal volume. They also tend to have fewer folds and wrinkles than vulcanized rubber dry suits or certain other urethane coated suits. This makes this type of suit very flexible and easy to use for swimming.

Due to the nature of the crushed neoprene material, suits made from this fabric have higher insulation values than dry suits made from vulca-

Taping the seam on a urethane dry suit.

This TLS suit features a self-donning design.

nized rubber or urethane coated fabric. This will allow you to use lighter dry suit underwear than you might normally select. Most divers find they can dive in waters 5 degrees cooler than the rating of their underwear when they wear a crushed neoprene suit.

One of the few drawbacks of crushed neoprene material is that to make permanent repairs, the material must be completely dry. The suits themselves are also a bit heavier than some of the lighter weight urethane and tri-laminate suits. However, for the diver who dives hard, such as a wreck diver or professional diver, crushed neoprene material is probably one of the best choices for a dry suit.

Unlike other dry suit materials, dry suits made from crushed neoprene material just seem to get better with age. The material becomes even more flexible and comfortable, like an old pair of blue jeans. Dry suits made from crushed neoprene material last a long time. Some divers have used crushed neoprene suits for over 10 years, with over 1000 dives. Like any other suit, storage and maintenance are critical factors in determining suit life.

DUI markets several crushed neoprene dry suits. Crushed neoprene material is patented by DUI.

Urethane Coated Fabric Dry Suits

Dry suits made from urethane backed nylon fabric became quite popular during the 1980's. Urethane is a synthetic material that creates a waterproof barrier when it is properly applied to nylon. Dry suits made from this material are commonly referred to as "pack cloth", or more correctly "polyurethane laminate" dry suits.

Nylon fabric is normally graded according to a rating system known as "denier". Generally speaking, the higher the denier number, the heavier the fabric. For example, 420 denier nylon is heavier than 210 denier nylon. This heavier fabric is more resistant to abrasion, but it is heavier in weight and less flexible.

To assemble a urethane fabric dry suit, the material is cut to the pattern and stitched together. To produce a watertight seam the joint must be sealed with a heat tape machine that welds a urethane tape over the seam. This type of dry suit is common because it is relatively easy to manufacture, and less expensive.

In a more complex assembly procedure, all of the seams are folded twice and then stitched. Although this method requires more labor and is more expensive, it produces a reliable seam.

Urethane coated fabrics are used to make some of the most light weight dry suits. The material is reasonably flexible.

Some nylon fabrics have little or no stretch. This is an important consideration in the design of a dry suit made from this material. In order to provide the room a diver needs to get into or out of a suit, and freedom of movement in the water, there must be enough excess fabric to compensate for this lack of stretch. This is one of the reasons why certain dry suits fit the way they do, i.e., loose and baggy.

The estimated life span of a dry suit made from urethane coated nylon material is approximately five to seven years of regular diving activity. When the urethane starts to break down this will show up as cracking in the material. When a suit delaminates early in its life it is usually because the material did not bond properly when it was manufactured.

Urethane/nylon suits include those manufactured by OS Systems, Seatec, DUI, and Harveys.

TLS Dry Suits

TLS is an abbreviation for *tri-laminate suit*. The TLS material was originally developed in Great Britain for NATO to use in chemical protective suits. It proved to be such an excellent gas and liquid proof barrier that it became evident it would make an excellent dry suit.

The layers in TLS material are tightly woven nylon with a layer of butyl rubber in between. TLS suits are stitched and the seams are sealed. As with other coated nylon fabrics, good seam construction is essential.

TLS suits are among the lightest weight yet strongest types of dry suits. The material is highly resistant to deterioration from smog and ozone.

TLS suits are quick and easy to repair. The suit is easily patched if punctured. The estimated life of a TLS suit is between five and seven years of active diving.

TLS suits are manufactured by Typhoon and DUI.

Vulcanized Rubber Dry Suits

Vulcanized rubber dry suits have been around for many years. The majority of these suits are made from a combination of natural and a synthetic rubber known as *EPDM*.

Vulcanized rubber is an excellent dry suit material. It dries quickly and can be patched in much the same way that you repair an inner tube or inflatable boat.

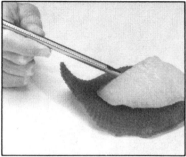

Raw rubber used to make vulcanized rubber dry suits.

Vulcanized rubber dry suits must be made from the right combination of materials. Without sufficient synthetics, the suits are prone to ozone attack and rapid deterioration. In addition, the material will be too elastic, allowing too much stretch.

It takes the right combination of materials to keep a vulcanized rubber suit from "ballooning" when inflated. The amount of stretch in the suit is primarily a function of the lining inside.

The inside of a vulcanized rubber dry suit is normally covered with a soft fabric. This makes it easier to dress into the suit. The fabric also provides a surface where moisture produced by your body will condense.

Manufacturing a vulcanized rubber dry suit is a bit different from the other suits described thus far. The seams of these suits are actually fused together under heat and pressure. If you look at the inside of these suits you will see that they are stitched along the seams, but this is only to hold them together prior to vulcanization.

To build a suit, the rubber coated fabric is cut into panels, stitched together, and pulled onto an aluminum mannequin. To ensure watertight seams, the seams of the suit should be taped after the suit is on the mannequin. This is the preferred method for manufacturing this type of dry suit. It results in more consistent sizing with less variation between suits. The quality of the finished suit is better.

Stitching a vulcanized rubber suit together prior to placing it on a mannequin.

Applying the tape to a vulcanized rubber dry suit prior to vulcanization. The legs of the mannequins can be seen in the background.

Although vulcanized rubber suits have good stretch, they usually fit most divers rather loosely. The reason for this is that the manufacturing process for this type of suit is very expensive and most manufacturers offer no more than four or five sizes.

While vulcanized rubber suits can be "customized", all of the tailoring occurs after the suit is manufactured. A skilled technician can alter a vulcanized rubber suit to fit almost any diver.

Vulcanized rubber suits that have been customized will have additional seams in them wherever the technician added or removed material. Divers who are concerned with fashion may not find this type of suit as attractive after alterations have been performed.

Some suits are made from vulcanized rubber material, but are not vulcanized as a suit to fuse the seams. Instead, the vulcanized material is merely glued together.

Vulcanized rubber dry suits are available in a variety of thicknesses; from very light material through extremely heavy material designed for commercial diving. The heavier the material, the more abrasion the suit can withstand. Vulcanized rubber dry suits are normally supplied with latex seals. Although it is possible to glue foam neoprene to this material, it takes many coats of glue to achieve a good bond.

Removing a rack of vulcanized rubber suits from the autoclave after heat treatment.

Final pressure test of a vulcanized rubber suit prior to shipment.

Selecting a Dry Suit to Fit You

If you are buying a new dry suit, you should put on the bulkiest dry suit underwear you anticipate using before you don the suit. This is very important, especially if the suit fits you snug.

Once you have the suit zipped up, test to see if you have complete movement in the suit. You should be able to freely squat, bend, kick, and reach. If your movement is hampered in any way the suit is probably too tight. It is better to have a dry suit that is a little bit loose than one that is too tight.

This Nokia Lady suit is a vulcanized rubber dry suit. It is the only vulcanized rubber suit that is specifically designed to fit women.

Chapter 5

Dry Suit Valves

Dry suit valves vary greatly in type and performance. The placement, construction, age, and design of the valves on your suit will directly affect your ability to control the air in your suit. A good set of valves can make a big difference in your diving enjoyment.

Like the dry suit material itself, most dry suit valves are made by specialized manufacturers. Some of the key makers of dry suit valves include Apeks and A.P. Valves in England, GSD in Italy, White's in Canada, SI Tech and Poseidon in Sweden. Just as dry suit zippers may appear on competing manufacturer's suits, the same dry suit valves may also be found on several different brands of suits. Yet while they appear outwardly the same, they may be manufactured to different specifications.

There are a number of types of dry suit valves that appear on contemporary dry suits. A dry suit inflator valve allows you to put air into your dry suit. Some manufacturers also refer to this type of valve as an "inlet valve". A dry suit exhaust valve will let air out of the suit. Certain manufacturers will refer to this type of valve as an "outlet valve".

Some manufacturers have added small additional exhaust valves to their suits on the wrists or ankles. These valves are appropriately known as "wrist valves", "cuff valves", or "ankle valves". They will not flow as much air as a regular exhaust valve. However, they will allow the diver to vent the dry suit from awkward positions.

Most dry suit exhaust valves today are known as "automatic exhaust valves". Although this is a commonly used term, it is not entirely correct. The valves will exhaust "automatically", provided the valves are at the highest point on the dry suit.

Assuming the dry suit exhaust valve is mounted on the left upper arm, the proper position for venting automatic exhaust valves is for the diver to be upright with his/her arm bent at the elbow, and raised at the elbow, hand down. With correct adjustment and positioning, hands free operation is possible. Most of these valves have a manual over-ride feature. (Proper dry suit diving techniques are covered thoroughly in Chapter 10.)

Another type of dry suit exhaust is the push-to-dump valve. This valve will vent only when you push down on either a button in the valve or the valve body itself.

In discussing the force required to operate a particular valve we will use the term "pounds force". This is abbreviated as "pounds$_f$", and is a measure of the force required to compress the spring in the valve. It is not realistic to use pounds per square inch, since some divers may use only a finger tip while other divers will use the palm of their hand. This results in a variation in the surface area of the valve button or head involved in its operation.

While some manufacturers claim that their exhaust valves will dump air faster than their inflator valve can supply it, in the real world this is not always true. In most cases when an inflator valve sticks it is essential to disconnect the inflator hose, while simultaneously venting from the exhaust. It may also be necessary to open the wrist or neck seal to control the ascent.

In this chapter, we will discuss the different types of dry suit valves most commonly encountered. Chapter 11 will include maintenance procedures for each of these valves. There are other valves available, but they are far less common. We have also purposely omitted valves that are no longer in production such as Henderson, Omega, Delphi, and Orion.

A.P. Valves

A.P. Valves is an English manufacturer of valves and buoyancy compensators. Their B.C.'s are extremely popular throughout Great Britain. A.P. Valves makes a small valve that can be mounted on the wrist of any dry suit. The valve is a non-adjustable automatic exhaust valve. In the U.K. these valves are commonly referred to as "cuff dumps".

The valve has a sealed body, so the flapper cannot be replaced. Once the flapper starts to leak the valve must be discarded and a new valve installed. The A.P. valve is designed to seal with an inner and outer gasket.

Apeks

Another British firm that manufactures dry suit valves is Apeks. In business since 1972, in addition to dry suit valves Apeks also manufactures a variety of scuba regulators, tank valves and manifolds, as well as other diving and medical equipment. Apeks manufactures all their products in-house.

The Apeks inflator valve is designed like most dry suit inflators. The body is made from a sturdy plastic material. The inflator button can easily be operated by a gloved hand. This design is known as a "plug valve". Other plug valves include S.I. Tech's and White's'.

The force required to operate the Apeks inflator is 5 pounds$_f$ of pressure. The maximum flow rate for this valve is just under 6 cubic feet of air per minute.

Like other dry suit inflators, the low pressure hose connects with a fitting that has a sliding outer sleeve that locks into position. It is important to use the inflator hose that is supplied with the valve. While other hoses may

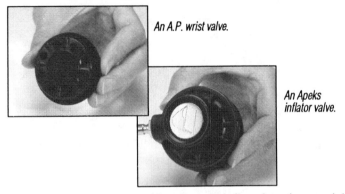

An A.P. wrist valve.

An Apeks inflator valve.

fit, they may have a much larger orifice that will inflate the suit too quickly. This situation could lead to an uncontrolled ascent.

When you turn the air on to your regulator, the inflator hose pressurizes but no air will escape. Connecting the hose to the valve engages a pin that opens the flow of air to the valve, but no air enters the suit until the valve button itself is depressed. This is the way most dry suit valves and B.C. inflators operate.

Apeks' dry suit exhaust valve is one of the better performing valves. It vents air quickly and easily. The valve is very easy to disassemble and clean. Like most other automatic valves, the Apeks valve has an adjustable back pressure spring. By adjusting the valve head you control the opening pressure of the valve and therefore the amount of air that is trapped in the suit.

The body of the valve is made of injection molded plastic. The springs and assembly screws are stainless steel. All Apeks valves are designed to mount with silicone caulk.

The Apeks valve has been designed as an "automatic exhaust valve". In a normal ascent situation, air migrates to the upper part of the suit. If the valve is located high on the upperarm when the diver lifts his left elbow to the

An Apeks exhaust valve.

A GSD inflator valve.

highest point, the air vents out through the valve. The air inside the suit actually lifts the valve away from the diver's body.

The amount of air that the dry suit will hold can be adjusted by turning the head of the valve that adjusts the back pressure setting. The top of the valve rotates with a ratchet motion. Turning the valve "in", or clockwise, will increase the back pressure saftely causing the suit to trap more air. Turning the valve "out", or counterclockwise, will allow the valve to vent more freely. The valve turns only one complete revolution from fully open to minimum exhaust.

The Apeks exhaust valve may also be vented manually by pushing on the top of the valve body. This action overrides the automatic exhaust features. This is helpful in the event the suit is over-inflated.

One of the most vital features in the Apeks design is the bottom of the valve, inside the suit. Air enters the valve body through a series of openings in the sides of the valve, rather than straight through the bottom of the valve. This is important, especially if the valve is vented manually.

When the valve is operated manually, the diver pushes the top of the valve down against his arm. This compresses the valve against the dry suit underwear.

With some older valves, the underwear can actually block the opening in the valve and prevent air from escaping from the suit. By designing the Apeks valve so that the air enters through the side, when the valve is pushed down by hand the air can still escape. All dry suit valves should have a stand-off similar to this. The force required to manually operate this valve is approximately 5.5 pounds. Apeks valves have been used on suits distributed by Typhoon and Parkway.

GSD

GSD is an Italian manufacturer of diving equipment. Although GSD gear is not widely distributed in the United States, they make a variety of equipment. All GSD valves are very rugged, made from chromed brass and injection molded plastic. This inlet valve is a "pilot valve", which means that once the air starts flowing through the valve, the air flow will become faster as the volume increases. The negative side of this design is that all pilot valves are very sensitive to any foreign matter and can easily jam shut.

The GSD inflator valve is large and easy to operate. The surface area of the inflator button is big. When you push the button, the travel is very short and air flow is almost immediate. The force required to operate this valve is 3 pounds$_f$. A maximum flow rate of 5.5 cubic feet of air per minute is possible with this valve.

A GSD push-to-dump valve.

The GSD push-to-dump valve will only exhaust air when you push the button in the center of the valve. As soon as you release the button the valve will not vent.

The GSD automatic exhaust valve is similar in appearance to the GSD

A GSD automatic exhaust valve.

push-to-dump valve. However, the automatic exhaust has a higher profile. You can also identify the GSD automatic exhaust by the arrows printed on the top of the valve. The GSD automatic exhaust turns exactly 1 1/2 turns from fully open to the minimum exhaust. DUI has used GSD valves on their suits for several years.

Poseidon Valves

Poseidon valves are from Sweden and appear on the Unisuit and Parkway suits. They have changed somewhat from their original design when the suit was first introduced.

The Poseidon inflator valve is a beefy valve. It uses a unique inflation hose connector that will only fit the Poseidon valve. The inflation button is large and recessed. The valve is made from chromed brass, plastic, and stainless steel. To start air flow through the valve it requires the diver to apply 10 pounds$_f$ to the button. Once the air is flowing, a maximum flow of 6.5 cubic feet of air per minute is possible. This is among the highest flow rates for a dry suit valve.

The Poseidon exhaust valve is another push-to-dump device. The button is recessed and requires a firm action with 12 pounds$_f$ to operate the

The Poseidon inflator valve.

The Poseidon exhaust valve.

valve. The valve is made from rubber, plastic, and stainless steel.

S.I. Tech

S.I. Tech is owned by Stig Insulan, one of the co-designers of the Viking suit. In the past, this Swedish company was known as S.I. Produkter.

S.I. Produkter originally made valves, and the mannequins for molding dry suits, exclusively for Viking. Their special agreement with Viking was dissolved in 1989. Insulan and his company then designed valves and mannequins for the dry suit market on a world wide basis. Although the S.I. Tech valves are still used on Viking suits, many dry suit manufacturers in different countries use products from S.I. Tech.

S.I. Tech makes several different types of inflators, but only one exhaust valve. The inflators are designed for different diving applications. The S.I. Tech Sport Inflator used on the Viking Sport dry suits is a unique design. The main parts of the valve are actually in the low pressure hose fitting.

The other half of the mechanism mounts on the suit itself. The mechanism on the suit connects to a special rubber mandrel. The back side of the valve seals with a Teflon® gasket inside the suit. Without this gasket the valve will leak. The components of the valve are injection molded plastic, stainless steel, and chromed brass.

The inflator button is square and mounted on the side of the valve. By pushing on the inflator button you actually compress a pin in the hose fitting. This starts the flow of air into your suit.

Although there is a check valve in the S.I. Tech Sport valve, if you use your suit for snorkeling, the mechanism on the suit should be plugged. S.I. Tech supplies a plug with every valve for this purpose. Without the plug in position there is a good chance the valve will leak and water will enter your dry suit.

The S.I. Tech Sport valve was originally designed to disengage itself automatically in the event you ditched your scuba unit. With a slight tug, the fitting will pop out of the valve head. While most older valves will do this, once the plastic is a bit worn, new valves may not disengage as easily. In addition, even an older valve may not detach itself when the diver is in certain positions.

To disengage an S.I. Tech sport hose from the valve body, you need to pinch the two sides of the valve that face the ends of the valve button. The hose can then easily disengage itself from the valve body.

S.I. Tech also manufactures two more conventional inflators. One requires a special hose fitting that is only available from Viking and DUI in the U.S., while the other uses the sleeve lock fitting that accompanies most power inflators.

The S.I. Tech Standard inflator was designed to be used on dry suits used by professional divers. It is a heavy duty valve that will withstand a lot of abuse. Like the S.I. Tech Sport Valve, the S.I. Tech Standard valve mounts on a special rubber mandrel on the Viking suit. Viking installs this valve on their PRO and heavy duty suits as standard, while DUI offers this valve as an option.

The hose connector on the S.I. Tech Standard valve comes in two configurations. Both are similar to the sleeve lock design found on the majority of dry suit inflators, but they only fit the S.I. Tech Standard valve. The older version is designed with two "wings" that stick out on either side. This makes it very easy to disconnect, even when wearing thick gloves. However, this design also makes it possible for any equipment that hits the valve to disconnect it.

The new S.I. Tech Standard hose connector is a round, sleeve lock style fitting. It is less prone to disconnect accidentally.

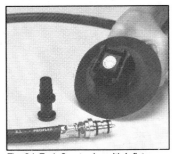

The S.I. Tech Sport valve with inflator hose and blanking plug for snorkeling.

The S.I. Tech Standard inflator button sticks up slightly above the top of the valve body. There are also flush and recessed buttons available. The valve requires 9 pounds$_f$ to start inflation. The valve will allow almost 7 cubic feet of air to flow per minute.

S.I. Tech also manufactures a new dry suit inflator that is more similar to the inflators offered by Apeks and White's, although the S.I. Tech inflator valve is

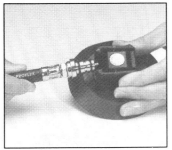

Pinch the end of the S.I. Tech Sport valve to disconnect the hose.

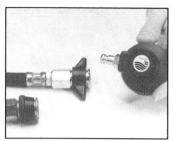

The S.I. Tech Standard inflator with the two low pressure hoses that connect to it.

S.I. Tech Inflator as used on DUI suits.

much smaller. This valve is found on current model DUI dry suits.

The S.I. Tech automatic exhaust valve is made from General Electric's Lexan®. The valve has passed through several generations, but all the designs are based on the same principles.

The valve swivels 1 1/2 turns from fully open to its minimum opening, and has a smooth operation. S.I. Tech valves have a high standoff that helps prevent them from blockage by dry suit underwear during manual operation.

S.I. Tech exhaust valves are used by both Viking and DUI. Although the valves are identical in appearance, those supplied by DUI come with a lighter spring to allow them to vent easier. The Viking version requires 6 pounds$_f$ to operate manually.

White's

White's valves are made in Canada. They are almost identical in appearance and operation to the Apeks valves.

The White's inflator valve has a large inflator button and is very easy to operate. The valve is made from chromed brass, injection molded plastic, and stainless steel, and will flow up to just over 6 cubic feet of air per minute. The inflator button requires 7 pounds$_f$ to operate the valve.

The White's exhaust valve is an automatic exhaust valve. It turns approximately 7/8 of a turn from fully open to its minimum opening. Manual operation requires 6.5 pounds$_f$

Dry Suit Valve Locations

The positions of the valves on your dry suit directly affect the buoyancy characteristics of your suit. Both the inflator valve and the exhaust valve need to be properly located in respect to the rest of your diving equipment.

The most common location for the dry suit inflator button is on the middle of the chest of the suit. This is a good location for several important reasons. First, it provides a solid base, your sternum (breast bone), to push the valve against to operate it. Secondly, this location does not interfere with most buoyancy compensators or other diving gear. Finally, it is a location that is easily reached whether you are right or left handed.

The only manufacturer that commonly mounts a valve in another location is Viking. The inflator valves on their PRO and heavy duty suits are positioned on the lower left side of the chest. For most divers, this valve hits on or below the lowest rib on the left side.

The rationale for Viking to mount their valves on the lower chest goes back many years and the reasons were good at that time. When the Viking suit was first designed, sport divers commonly wore horse collar style buoyancy compensators, rather than jacket style B.C.'s. With this arrangement, a diver could actually operate the inflator button on his suit with his elbow if both his hands were busy.

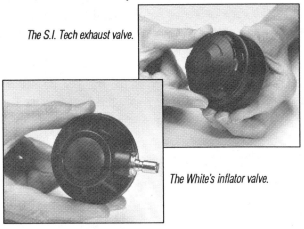

The S.I. Tech exhaust valve.

The White's inflator valve.

Viking heavy duty suits are frequently used by commercial divers with a variety of helmets. Since it is more economical to manufacture suits in quantity and attach special helmet yokes later, all Viking suits are vulcanized with the valve mandrels in their normal position. If a diver doesn't need or want the inflator valve the hole can be blanked off with a special plug.

If the inflator valve mandrel on a Viking heavy duty suit was located on the mid chest, it might interfere with certain heavy gear helmets that are still used in Europe. Even though very few of these helmets are used, it is still easier for Viking to manufacture suits with the standard valve in its original position.

Divers in the U.S. who use the Viking PRO or heavy duty suits should be careful to select a buoyancy compensator that does not cover the inflator valve. There have been several cases of accidental suit inflation where the buoyancy compensator pushed on the suit inflator and caused an uncontrolled ascent. Some professional diving harnesses can also interfere

The White's exhaust valve.

with the inflator valve depending upon the type of harness and the diver's physique.

If you don't want to replace your B.C., Viking can blank off your suit inflator and attach a second valve mandrel in another location on your suit. There is a nominal charge for this service.

Although some dry suit manufacturers position the exhaust valve on the diver's chest, the most common location for the valve is on your upper arm. With the valve located on the chest it is not possible to get the excess air out of the suit. Notice we say, "the excess air", because with today's valves it is not possible to get all the air out of the suit. There will always be some air trapped inside the suit unless the suit is flooded.

Another disadvantage to mounting the exhaust valves on the chest is that this forces you to assume an upright position in the water to vent the suit. If the exhaust valve is mounted on the arm you can vent the suit, as you continue to swim, by rolling on your right side. From the above explanation, it is easy to see that the best position for the exhaust valve is on your upper arm.

Dry Suit Valve Performance

While dry suit valve manufacturers are careful to provide excellent quality control, the reality is that no two valves will perform identically. Dry suit valves, like automobiles or scuba regulators, are manufactured within a certain range of tolerances. When they are assembled, they are tested and the valves must perform within a certain range to be acceptable for safe diving. Other factors that will affect a valve's performance include the age of the valve, how well the valve has been maintained, the water temperature, and the gas used to fill the dry suit.

To test the efficiency of an exhaust valve, the pressure drop across the valve is measured. This test calculates the flow of gas from inside the suit to outside the suit. The higher the pressure drop, the less air is trapped inside the suit. Another way to think about this is that the higher the pressure drop, the faster the valve will vent. Ideally, a dry suit exhaust valve should vent as quickly as possible with the lowest change in pressure to help avoid an uncontrolled ascent.

Tests were conducted on 6 dry suit exhaust valves at a maximum flow rate of 5 cubic feet per minute. The two valves that exhaust the fastest are the White's and the S.I. Tech automatic exhaust valves. The two slowest valves are the Delphi and Poseidon valves.

Chapter 6

Dry Suit Undergarments

Without proper dry suit underwear, even the best dry suit will not keep you warm. Selecting the right dry suit underwear for your particular diving application is not hard, but it does require some knowledge and thought. There are many different types of dry suit underwear available. Each type of material has very different characteristics that will not only affect your warmth, but will also influence your buoyancy, mobility, and comfort.

The smart dry suit diver thinks in terms of *insulation strategies* for particular dives. Just as there is not one wetsuit that will keep you comfortable under all diving conditions, there is not one set of dry suit underwear that will be applicable to all divers under all situations. By developing a proper insulation strategy you will be able to put together the proper selection of dry suit undergarments for any dive.

Our goal in developing an insulation strategy is to maintain the diver in *thermal balance.* The ideal situation is one where you are neither too hot or too cold. Your should be at a comfortable temperature when you dive.

Most people who participate in cold weather sports topside are familiar with the concept of *layering.* The terms refers to wearing several different garments that will keep you warm, rather than one single garment.

When you dress in layers of clothing, you can remove some of the garments to adjust for changes in the weather or your exercise rate. While it is not possible to remove garments underwater, it is possible to adjust our insulation <u>before</u> the dive, based upon, our individual physiology, the water temperature, and, our planned diving activity (exercise rate).

As we have mentioned before, a dry suit works on the principle of passive insulation. The dry suit underwear traps a layer of air. The combination of air compartments in the underwear slows the heat transfer from your body to the water. For two sets of underwear made from the same material, the thicker set will trap more air and keep you warmer. However besides you must consider the aterial the underweaar is make from.Just because a set of underwear of one type is thicker than another type does not necessarily mean it will be warmer. It all depends upon the efficiency of the material from which the underwear is constructed. The ideal dry suit undergarment is the thinnest design that traps the most air in the smallest spaces. Certain materials, such as Thinsulate®, have much higher insulation efficiency than others.

The efficiency of a dry suit undergarment is calculated in terms of a unit of measurement known as "Clo". A Clo unit is the amount of thermal insulation that is required to maintain an "average" resting man in thermal balance in an air environment where the temperature is 70 degrees Fahrenheit, the relative humidity is less than 50%, and the air movement is 20 feet per minute. These conditions approximate what we might call "room temperature".

From another perspective, the "average" person is comfortable when naked at a temperature of 86 degrees Fahrenheit. A Clo unit represents the amount of insulation required for the 16 degree drop between the comfortable nude resting temperature and 70 degrees Fahrenheit.

As a further point of reference, a 1/4 inch thick wetsuit has a Clo value of approximately 1.8 Clo at the surface. However, at a depth of 100 feet, after the suit has been compressed, the Clo value of the same suit is only approximately 0.25 Clo.

In any dry suit, you will usually perspire to a certain degree, even during dives in relatively cold water. This moisture from your body will condense against the cold surface of the suit. How your dry suit underwear responds to this moisture will greatly determine how comfortable you will be in your suit. If the underwear soaks up this wetness you will feel cold and clammy inside your suit.

In this chapter we will compare different types of dry suit undergarments and provide you with the information to make predictions regarding your insulation needs. However, it is important to realize that each diver's insulation needs are different. Two divers of the same size may have very different thermal protection needs.

We caution you that our recommendations for insulation are guidelines only. They will provide the new dry suit diver with a starting point for selecting insulation. However, it is up to you to experiment and see what feels best to you. You may need more or less insulation than is recommended in the tables in the appendix.

CAUTION:

Different manufacturers have used different systems for rating the thermal efficiency of their garments. It is recommended that before accepting a manufacturer's rating for your personal use that you check the following:

a) Check the basis for the rating. Ask the manufacturer what basis was used for the rating. Some manufacturers use more conservative rating systems than others. Remember that each person has a different heat production rate and heat loss rate.

b) Check the overall thickness of the insulation under compression. A quick way to do this is to just compress the underwear between your thumb and forefinger. A more accurate measurement can be achieved by preparing two squares of thin, stiff material, such as Plexiglass, measuring two inches by two inches square. Place one piece on either side of a piece of underwear and lay the whole assembly on a table. Place a 2 pound weight on the outside square. Measure the thickness of the underwear material between the two squares. Under these conditions you have the equivalent of approximately .5 P.S.I. suit compression, which is roughly equivalent to the pressure the underwear experiences during normal diving conditions.

Dry Suit Underwear is Available in Many Styles

While the material used in the construction of your dry suit underwear will have the biggest influence on your warmth, there are many other factors that will affect your diving comfort. There are also certain other features that will make your diving more convenient.

Some divers prefer undergarments assembled as one piece jumpsuits, while other divers prefer a separate jacket and pants. This is a matter or personal preference. Although you may add other pieces of underwear, such as a polypropylene liner or fleece vest, the most versatile dry suit underwear is a farmer john style pants with a jacket on top. This design allows for the greatest freedom of movement and adjustment.

Pockets are a feature that aren't essential to your comfort, but make your diving more convenient. Most better quality dry suit undergarments are equipped with pockets.

Make sure you don't put anything in your pockets that can be damaged by pressure, or that could damage your dry suit when the suit compresses. For example, if your keys are bulky or sharp they could cut through your underwear and possibly your suit during the course of your dive. Similarly,

Viking open cell underwear.

Dry suit underwear from Scubapro.

Photo courtesy of Scubapro.

items that could conceivably implode, leak, or cut into you, such as pens or cigarette lighters are best left topside during the dive if possible.

When you evaluate dry suit underwear take a good look at the boots that come with the garment. The boots should be thick enough to provide adequate insulation, especially when you are in an upright position underwater. Yet, at the same time, they must be loose enough to allow for proper blood circulation.

Whenever you are upright, you will feel more pressure on the lower part of your suit than on your chest and arms. This happens as the air in the lower part of your suit shifts as you change position. For this reason, the boots must be made from a material that will resist compression.

Another critical factor to consider is the material used to cover the bottom and sides of the underwear boots. This material should be skid resistant and waterproof. Underwear boots that absorb water as you walk on the deck of a dive boat become very uncomfortable during subsequent dives. At a minimum, the soles and sides of the boots should be covered with a material that is water resistant.

The fit of your dry suit underwear is as important as the fit of your dry suit. The underwear should not be restrictive. You should be able to freely bend, squat, kneel, kick, and climb a ladder. If you have difficulty performing any of these movements while wearing the underwear alone, they will be even more difficult after you put on a dry suit. Your dry suit underwear must fit you properly.

Open Cell Foam Underwear

Open cell foam is a material that when examined in cross section has the appearance of a sponge. The material most commonly used is a polyurethane. When it is used in dry suit underwear it is normally laminated with a nylon material. The material is cut into panels and stitched together.

Open cell foam underwear is reasonably resistant to compression. This helps it to maintain a fairly consistent air layer in the suit under pressure. The Clo rating for open cell foam underwear at depth is approximately 1.2Clo.

Dry suit undergarments made from open cell foam are very light in weight. The material is very flexible but has virtually no stretch. Given the nature of the material, dry suit underwear cut from this material tends to fit quite loose and baggy. Many divers refer to the appearance of this underwear as the "dough-boy look".

Although open cell foam underwear will keep you reasonably warm if it becomes damp, it will not keep you warm if it becomes soaked. In addition, once this underwear becomes wet, it takes a long time to dry.

Open cell foam underwear may be washed with soap in a washing machine. You'll want to launder your underwear whenever it becomes wet with salt water, or when it begins to smell from sweat. If you only need to get rid of salt you can wash it with water alone. You can also use a capful of bleach by itself during a wash cycle to get rid of any odor.

When you wash open cell foam underwear, air drying may take 24 hours or more. You can dry the material in a dryer, but only on air dry or very low heat. Even in a dryer, open cell foam underwear takes quite a while to dry. Do not leave this material in a dryer unattended because it can catch on fire quite easily. You can also speed the drying of this material by spinning it over your head to get rid of excess water if you are on a boat with no dryer.

Open cell foam underwear may lose all of its buoyancy when the dry suit is completely flooded. Also, open cell foam underwear tends to require more weight for the diver to achieve neutral buoyancy than certain other types of dry suit underwear for equal thermal protection.

Open cell foam underwear is normally supplied as a one piece garment with attached boots. Although the material used on the soles of the boots is water resistant it is not waterproof. If you are a boat diver and remove your dry suit between dives, you should avoid stepping on wet areas of the deck while wearing just your underwear. The boots will readily soak up water if you don't pay attention to where you put your feet.

Viking is the primary manufacturer of open cell foam underwear.

Thinsulate®

Thinsulate® is a synthetic material that was developed by the 3M Corporation during the mid 70's. It is an exceptionally light weight material that has excellent insulation characteristics.

Thinsulate® is a "microfiber".

Cutting Thinsulate® material to make dry suit underwear.

There are a variety of different types of Thinsulate® for different applications. The only type that is acceptable for underwater use is Type "B". This material is "hydrophobic", which means that it repels water. Thinsulate® fibers absorb less than 1% by weight of water.

Thinsulate® is made from polyolefin microfibers. The 3M company supplies two different thicknesses of this material. Type B200 material comes in sheets that are .2 inches thick. This material has a value of .9 Clo. Type B400 is .4 inches thick and has a rating of 1.8Clo.

Manufacturers of dry suit underwear use Thinsulate® in combination with other materials to produce their undergarments. The Thinsulate® is normally sandwiched between layers of other material. For example, the outside of the garment will usually be a nylon taffeta to help the dry suit to slide easily over the undergarment. The inside of the underwear may be a synthetic polyester "fleece" for comfort against the skin. The additional layers of material may also increase the Clo rating of the garment.

The greatest advantage of Thinsulate® dry suit undergarments is that even if your dry suit leaks, Thinsulate® underwear still provides good insulation. While we do not recommend diving with a dry suit that has developed a leak, you will be much warmer with a Thinsulate® undergarment in this type of situation.

Thinsulate® batting is very dense. Any water that contacts Thinsulate® is broken up into very small droplets that are separated by these fibers. This action helps to prevent heat transfer since the water drops are not touching each other.

Booties made from Thinsulate® will absorb very little water, which is a big plus if you must remove your dry suit on a wet deck. Since the lower part of your dry suit usually suffers from the greatest compression, the consistent insulation provided by this material makes diving more comfortable.

Diving Unlimited International (DUI) uses Thinsulate® in their

Divewear dry suit underwear. They offer their garments in two temperature ratings; 50-65 degrees F and 35-50 degrees F. DUI uses a heavier layer of Thinsulate® on the torso and thinner material on the arms and legs for maximum flexibility.

Typhoon offers Thinsulate® underwear in two weights. Their light weight undersuit is provided in a 45-50 degrees F model. Their heavy weight undersuit is designed for water temperatures colder than 45 degrees F, but no lower limit is stated.

Ocean Bottoms/Mountain Tops uses Thinsulate® in combination with an aluminized polyethelene film known as Texolite®. They offer three different gar-

This one piece Thinsulate® jumpsuit is designed for 50-65 degree waters.

ments rated for 45-55 degrees F, 40-50 degrees F and a very heavy garment they rate for "long duration and extreme exposure conditions". No temperature range is provided for the heavy weight garment.

While Thinsulate® fibers repel water, they "love" oil. When you sweat, the oils from your body will accumulate in Thinsulate® underwear. Dirt will stick to this oil and water will be absorbed by the dirt. These factors combined will rob Thinsulate® of its efficiency. For this reason it is very important to launder your Thinsulate® underwear properly.

To properly launder Thinsulate® you must pay close attention to the care instructions provided with the particular garment you are using. Soap acts as a "wetting agent". Wetting agents allow the oils and dirt to be washed out of garments. If the soap is not totally removed during laundering it will dry inside the garment and remain as a wetting agent during your dives. Since Thinsulate® is designed to be hydrophobic this will reduce its capabilities.

If you use soap, use it sparingly and run the garment through three additional complete wash cycles without soap to remove all traces of the detergent. You can also use a 1/2 cap of bleach to remove any smell. Be sure to add the bleach after the washer is full to avoid damaging the material.

Follow the specific drying instructions for your garment. If no instructions are available, allow the garment to air dry on a plastic hanger. Remember that most synthetic fibers are affected by heat and Thinsulate® is no different. Drying Thinsulate® at a high temperature will cause the fibers to melt and reduce their effectiveness.

Many divers like to wear a liner underneath their dry suit undergarment.

Amron International manufactures this pile suit with boots.

Radiant Insulating Undergarments

Radiant insulating undergarments were originally developed for diving by Pat Baird at a company known as Underwave. The company no longer exists although similar garments are now manufactured by Baird for a company known as Ocean Bottoms/Mountain Tops.

As mentioned previously, an aluminized polyethelene film is just one of the components used in this type of underwear. The theory behind the use of the aluminized polyethylene film is that it provides a barrier to radiant heat loss. The value of radiant barrier insulation in diving has yet to be proven.

Radiant film, Texolite®, is only used in the RF45 garment and the RF27 garment. No Clo ratings are available for these garments.

Wooly Bears

The term "wooly bear" has been used in dry suit diving for many years. It is a generic term that is used to refer to any dry suit undergarment that is made from a synthetic pile. Today there are many different synthetic materials available, so it is important to know what material was used to make the garment you select.

Most of the early wooly bears were made from nylon. While the material was reasonably comfortable, it was not as pleasant to wear as some of the better fibers currently sold.

One of the major disadvantages of pile was that the material had a tendency to form balls of lint, or "pill", after laundering. These balls of lint would break loose from the surface of the underwear and find their way into the dry suit exhaust valve. Some divers who have used nylon wooly bears have had the exhaust valves on their suits jammed by the lint produced by the garment. When lint jams an exhaust valve shut it becomes impossible to vent the suit properly. When lint jams an exhaust valve open the suit will not hold air properly and the diver will get wet.

Many of the wooly bears today are made from polyester. Polyester has a nice feel against your skin and offers reasonable insulation. While some of the more expensive piles are quite comfortable to wear, they may not provide good insulation.

A vest can add extra insulation to your core.

A wooly bear made from 16 ounce polyester has an approximate value of 1.65 Clo depending upon the exact nature of the material. Polyester does not form lint like nylon. When polyester is wet it has very little insulation capability.

Most polyester undergarments can be easily laundered. Use warm water and a minimum amount of soap. Set your dryer to "no heat/air dry" or let the underwear dry on a plastic hanger.

Polypropylene Liners

A polypropylene or other mountaineering style liner can extend the temperature range of your dry suit underwear by as much as an additional 5 degrees F. The liner not only will add insulation, it will also help to wick moisture away from your body.

During the warmer summer months, a polypropylene liner and sweat suit may be sufficient insulation for some divers at water temperatures above 70 degrees F. Some divers even use their dry suit in the tropics with this light weight combination! If you use sweats be sure they are synthetic rather than cotton. Cotton sweats saturate easily and will conduct heat rapidly away from the body when wet.

Follow the care instructions for your particular garment when laundering.

Vests

Some dry suit undergarment manufacturers offer vests that will help extend the comfort range of their outfits. By insulating your torso, you provide vital protection to your core. Both DUI and Ocean Bottoms/Mountain Tops manufacture vests that can be worn over your dry suit underwear.

Chapter 7

Dry Suit Accessories

Dry suit accessories range from those items that are "nice to have", to those that are "essential" to dry suit diving. The more diving you do with your dry suit, the more you will appreciate the enjoyment these accessories will add to your diving.

Gloves & Mittens

There are two types of gloves used for dry suit diving, wet and dry. Wet gloves are ordinary wetsuit gloves. Wet mitts with three fingers are also available. Wet hand protection is adequate in cool water, but not in water temperatures much below 50 degrees F. Wetsuit gloves compress at depth, resulting in a loss of insulation. However, they are cheaper to buy than dry gloves.

The best wetsuit gloves are those available with a long gauntlet, providing there is a minimum of water circulation. The gauntlet is helpful because it also helps protect your dry suit wrist seal, by guarding it from objects that might puncture it.

Three fingered mitts offer greater cold water protection by decreasing the surface area of the fingers. They also tend to be thicker than the very thin neoprene used in wetsuit gloves. However, three finger mitts will decrease your ability to work with your hands, making it difficult to operate small camera controls.

In moderate temperature waters, gauntlet gloves offer adequate protection.

This diver is wearing a pair of dry three fingered mitts.

A simple pair of dry mitts with doughnut seals.

Dry gloves and dry mittens are manufactured in several different styles. Whether you use dry gloves or dry mittens they are usually designed to work with a set of cuff rings. "Doughnut seals" are the exception and they are also designed to be dry.

S.I. Tech cuff rings consist of two parts; an inner ring and an outer ring. The inner ring is usually made from a rigid, machined plastic. The outer ring is usually made from a more flexible rubber. There are many different dry glove systems available and the assembly procedures vary from manufacturer to manufacturer.

Like your dry suit, the dry gloves and mittens are designed to be worn with some type of insulating material. In most cases, a thin wool or synthetic liner is worn under the dry glove. The liner provides both insulation and protection from squeezes. Without a liner the dry gloves are extremely uncomfortable.

Some divers like to equalize the pressure in their dry gloves by inserting a piece of surgical tubing, or open cell foam, under the wrist seal of their suit. This allows air from the dry suit to enter the gloves. Equalizing the gloves eliminates any possibility of a squeeze on your hands.

There are two problems that can happen when you equalize the pressure in your gloves. First, if the gloves leak, for any reason, water can enter the suit through the opening created by the tube or foam. Secondly, as you return to the surface at the end of your dive you must be sure to keep your hands low, so that the air in the gloves can return to your suit and vent through the exhaust valve. If you forget to do this there is a possibility that as the air inside your gloves expands it will blow the glove off your hand.

Dry gloves obviously will keep your hands the warmest. They are highly recommended any time the water is colder than 50 degrees F. Whichever glove you choose, be sure you can operate all of your equipment and perform all emergency procedures with your gloves on.

Slip-On Knee Pads

If the knee pads on your dry suit aren't heavy enough to hold up to sustained wear, you may want to use slip-on knee pads for additional protection. Slip-on knee pads are usually made from the same material used on the soles of hard sole wetsuit boots. The material is very rugged. When this type of knee pad wears out it can be easily replaced.

Slip-on knee pads are especially appreciated by underwater photographers or any other diver who spends a lot of time kneeling on the bottom. Keep in mind that any material placed around the knee creates some resistance and can interfere with your swimming ability.

Relief Zipper

For male divers who do a lot of cold weather diving, where you don't remove your dry suit between dives, a relief zipper is a nice accessory. The relief zipper is designed to allow you to urinate on the surface, between dives, without removing your dry suit or underwear. Unfortunately, most dry suit designs do not accommodate the needs of female divers in this area.

Relief zippers are waterproof, pressure-proof zippers, just like the zipper used to enter your dry suit. They must be given the same care and maintenance your regular dry suit zipper requires.

Pockets

Pockets can be added to your dry suit in almost any location you desire. They are a handy place to store lens caps, shells, or other small items. The best time to have pockets installed is when you order a new suit, although they can almost always be installed later.

Pockets should be self-draining so that they won't hold water after you have surfaced. They must be located where they will not interfere with other equipment. Two popular locations for pockets are on the thigh or the chest.

Never put anything sharp in the pocket of your dry suit, particularly if the object is large and fills the pocket completely. Sharp objects could conceivably cut through the pocket and the dry suit itself.

Neck Ring Clamps

A neck ring clamp is a device used to attach temporary neck seals, or dry hoods, to a dry suit. This allows you to quickly change out neck seals that are damaged. It also permits you to use the same size dry suit with a variety of neck seals that have been trimmed to different sizes. This is especially convenient for search and rescue teams that may need to share suits.

The neck ring clamp is designed to capture a neck seal or dry hood between a steel clamp and a plastic ring. The plastic ring is assembled around the diver's neck. It snaps together with a positive action.

After the plastic ring is in position, the base neck seal on the suit is stretched over the ring. The base neck seal has a wide opening that will not seal on a diver's neck. The diver then dons a second neck seal that is properly sized for his or her neck. The metal clamp is then closed over the latex seals, compressing the seals against the plastic ring and forming a waterproof seal.

A neck ring clamp

A typical set of cuff rings.

Neck ring clamps should be carefully maintained and checked prior to each dive. Although these clamps are made from stainless steel, they can still corrode. If the clamp shows signs of heavy wear it should be replaced. If the clamp fails while the diver is underwater the neck seal can come off and the dry suit could flood completely.

Weight Distribution

Ankle weights are considered an optional dry suit accessory. They are not essential to dry suit diving.

For the beginning dry suit diver, ankle weights give a sense of security and control, like training wheels on a bicycle. They can help you to regain an upright position if you are upside down, and the air in your dry suit rushes to your feet. However, if you are properly weighted for dry suit diving, and have a minimal volume of air in your suit, you should not need ankle weights to control your buoyancy.

Some dry suit divers use ankle weights to help distribute some of the extra weight they require for dry suit diving. Ankle weights allow you to remove some of the weight from your belt. Since a heavy weight belt can cause lower back pain this may be beneficial.

Yet, by placing weights on the ankle at the end of the leg, this may, in itself, cause lower back pain. Each time you kick you must move the mass of the ankle weight. This stress demands more energy from the diver.

Ankle weights are not a necessity for dry suit diving.

A better alternative for distributing this additional weight may be to use a buoyancy compensator that is equipped with weight pockets and a weight release mechanism. If you put weights in your B.C., you should only use a B.C. that is specifically designed to handle them.

By placing weights in the B.C., you transfer the distribution of weights from around your waist to across your back when you are swimming, and onto your shoulders when you are standing. This is a much more comfortable arrangement. Some divers also use weights strapped to their thighs, appropriately known as "thigh weights". This allows you to adjust your trim or attitude, i.e., the angle that you swim through the water. Most divers swim in a head up attitude, with their feet much lower than their waist. A head up attitude can stir up silt if you are swimming close to the bottom.

In certain situations, such as cave diving or wreck diving, it may be more desirable to swim in a head down attitude, with the head lower than the feet. By using a weight system that allows you to adjust your trim you can assume the attitude that is best suited to the type of diving you are doing. If thigh weights are used they must never cover the knee or slip below the knee.

DUI has developed a new weight and trim system that is designed to be used by divers who have a high degree of technical competency. This new system will allows you to adjust your trim underwater and transfers a diver's weight load to their shoulders.

Buoyancy Compensators

Choosing a buoyancy compensator to use with a dry suit involves some important considerations regarding the placement of the valves on your dry suit. Valve location will affect both the ease with which you can don your B.C. and your access to the valves themselves.

Jacket style, non-adjustable buoyancy compensators, such as stabilizing jackets, can be difficult to don over a vulcanized rubber dry suit. The rugged material of the jacket does not slide easily over suits made from this

Most dry suit divers find they need a set of fins with a larger foot pocket than what they wear with a neoprene bootie.

This diver is wearing a buoyancy compensator equipped with weight pockets.

material. In addition, since the arm openings cannot be adjusted, it can be difficult to get an arm mounted exhaust valve through the jacket.

The easiest type of B.C. to use with a dry suit is one that has shoulder buckles that can be opened or closed. Jacket style adjustable buoyancy compensators put the buoyancy under your arms and tend to rotate you to an upright position.

The other important factor in B.C. selection is to ensure that none of the straps or bladder sections interfere with the operation of your dry suit valves. The B.C. must not cover any of the valves on your dry suit.

Many divers prefer low volume, back mounted style buoyancy compensators for use with their dry suits. Whatever B.C. you select, it should be capable of providing enough lift to give you positive buoyancy even when your dry suit is completely flooded and all of your other gear is still in place.

For surface swimming in your dry suit, it is much more comfortable to use your buoyancy compensator to establish positive buoyancy than to use your dry suit. When your dry suit is inflated enough to make you buoyant on the surface there will usually be excess pressure on the neck seal. This can be very uncomfortable.

In reality, most divers probably need no more than 20 pounds of lift from a buoyancy compensator for dry suit diving. Even if your suit floods completely you should not need much more buoyancy than this to establish positive buoyancy at the surface. Although a complete flood is rare, all the dry suit manufacturers recommend that a buoyancy compensator should be worn with a dry suit under all diving conditions.

Fins

Most divers find they need a fin with a larger foot pocket than what they normally use with a wetsuit bootie. The combination of dry suit boot and dry suit underwear is quite bulky.

You may also want to add a short pull strap to your fin strap to help get them off after diving. Some fin straps are equipped with tabs for this purpose. However, with certain types of fins, it can be quite difficult to get the strap over a bulky dry suit boot. A short lanyard of braided nylon attached to the back of your fin strap can make this task much easier.

Necklace Ring

While you are on the surface, between dives, you may find your dry suit neck seal to be a bit snug. However, if the neck seal is properly adjusted

To relieve pressure on the neck seal while topside, you may want to use a necklace ring.

Necklace rings are made from plastic tubing. They snap together loosely around your neck at the level of your neck seal. By folding the neck seal over the necklace ring you pull the neck seal away from your neck.

Using the necklace ring also allows heat and water vapor to escape from your dry suit. Just be sure to remove

A necklace ring will relieve the pressure of the neck seal between dives.

the necklace ring and properly adjust your neck seal before you enter the water.

Low Pressure Swivel Adaptors

If you own an older regulator, the first stage may not have enough low pressure ports to accommodate your dry suit and your other low pressure hoses. If you use an octopus regulator, you will need at least 4 low pressure ports to handle your dry suit, B.C., octopus, and primary regulator. Be sure to check the length of all of the hoses to make sure they are not under strain when you are fully suited up.

The low pressure swivel adaptor may also be required even if you have enough ports, just to conform to the different angles your hoses must take. For example, if all your low pressure ports are clustered on one side of your first stage, you may not be able to make certain connections without kinking the hoses. If you must bend a hose to make a connection you need a low pressure adaptor.

Some older regulators will require you to use a swivel "T" connector for all of your low pressure connections.

In most cases you may also be able to swivel the inflator valve on your dry suit to accept an inflator hose that must come from a particular side. It is usually possible to loosen the valve and turn it until the valve head is at the proper angle to meet the hose. This modification should be performed by a qualified dry suit dealer or repair facility. However, we do not recommend changing the angle of the valve connection recommended by the manufacturer. An improper angle can stress the hose and may lead to premature failure.

Be aware that some valves are sealed to certain dry suits with silicone rubber. If you swivel a valve and break the silicone sealant the suit will leak. See your dry suit dealer to have this service performed.

Chapter 8

Setting Up Your Dry Suit Systems

Once you have obtained all of the components of your dry suit system, it is still necessary to set them up correctly. You can have the best dry suit system available, but without proper harmony between all the pieces it will not function well.

Adjusting Dry Suit Seals

One of the most basic tasks in setting up your dry suit system is to make sure the seals on your suit are adjusted properly for you. If you don't take the time to do this, the seals on your suit will be extremely uncomfortable and possibly even dangerous. See Chapter 4 for complete information on adjusting dry suit seals.

Regulator/Inflator Hose Geometry

Your dry suit inflator valve should only be connected to one of the low pressure ports on your regulator's first stage. Never connect the low pressure hose to any port marked "H.P." (high pressure). Connecting the hose to a high pressure port could cause it to fail, injuring you and people around you. If you are unsure of how to do this, see your instructor or dealer and have them assist you.

If you do connect your dry suit inflator hose yourself, use the correct size wrench on the inflator hose and the plug in your regulator. Adjustable wrenches tend to slip, and can round the corners on brass fittings. This can make it difficult to achieve the proper torque in connecting a fitting or removing it later.

All of the components of your dry suit system must work together.

When you connect your dry suit inflator hose to your first stage, take a careful look at the angle and route it must take to connect to your suit inflator valve. It is very important that you do not stress or kink the hose to make the connection. Stretching the hose, or bending it to the point where it kinks, will create problems that could lead the inflator hose to fail. The hose must be long enough to comfortably reach your inflator.

Dry suit inflator hoses should follow a gently curving path to connect to your suit inflator valve. To achieve the correct angle it may be necessary to disconnect some of your other hoses and change the ports where they have been attached. Make sure all of the low pressure hoses are only connected to ports that are marked "L.P." (low pressure).

Some regulators are equipped with a special large bore, low pressure outlet for the second stage supply hose. In this situation, there may only be one low pressure outlet available for mating to the second stage hose.

Your regulator may have a sufficient number of low pressure ports, but with certain regulator and tank valve combinations the angles at which they join may make it difficult to properly route your low pressure hose. If this is the case, you may need a low pressure adaptor or swivel "T" to make acceptable connections.

Another important consideration may be the length of your low pressure hose. Again, certain valve and regulator combinations may make a long, low pressure inflator hose desirable. Check with your dealer regarding the availability of extra-long inflator hoses. Certain manufacturers do offer this type of optional equipment.

Finally, you may also be able to rotate the low pressure inflator valve on your suit to a more comfortable angle. However, before you loosen the mount nut on the inside of your suit, check the valve to see how it seals to the suit itself. Also, if you turn the inflator so that the hose connects at a different angle, check to see that you can still disconnect the hose easily

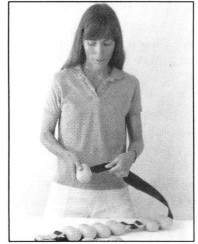

when you have the suit on. This is essential during an emergency.

On most vulcanized rubber dry suits, the valves are mounted with a simple gasket that allows you to rotate the valve any time you need to do it. You just loosen the nut, turn the valve, and tighten the nut again. The valve should be tested for proper operation after rotation.

If the valve is not properly rotated and retightened, particularly with the Viking PRO valve, it will either allow the suit to flood, or the valve will free-flow. The spring inside the valve must engage the nipple on both pieces of the valve body.

On other dry suits, such as the DUI TLS suits, the valves are mounted with silicone sealant (RTV). If the valve must be rotated, it should be completely removed from the suit and the old silicone must be removed.

After you have cleaned the valve and removed all of the old silicone, new silicone must be applied for the valve to seal. Most silicone sealant requires several hours for it to set up properly. Once the silicone has cured the suit should be leak tested to make sure it is watertight. See Chapter 12 for instructions on how to leak test your suit.

Estimating Your Weight Requirements

With most combinations of dry suits and underwear you will need anywhere from 4 to 10 pounds of additional weight compared to the weight you would wear with a full 1/4 inch wetsuit. How much weight you will need will depend upon your personal buoyancy, the type of dry suit you are using, the type of dry suit underwear you are wearing, the fit of your dry suit, and the type of tank you use. Some divers are actually able to wear less weight with their dry suit system than with a 1/4 inch thick wetsuit.

The most important point to keep in mind is that all else being equal, your weight requirements will change most dramatically when you change the amount of underwear you use with your suit. This is particularly important if you dive in a location where you use an entirely different set of underwear during different seasons.

All scuba cylinders become more buoyant as the air inside the tank is consumed. This buoyancy varies depending upon the cylinder material and the volume. Check the manufacturer's specifications for your cylinder to see how the buoyancy changes from the time the tank is full until it is empty. Take this amount of additional weight with you when you dive your dry suit for the first time.

You should initially test your buoyancy in a swimming pool or other shallow, confined body of water. Of course, if you test your buoyancy in fresh water you will need a few more pounds to dive in salt water. To adjust for the change from fresh to salt water add weight in the following amount:

Diver's weight	Additional Weight
125 lbs.	4 lbs.
155 lbs.	5 lbs.
186 lbs.	6 lbs.
217 lbs.	7 lbs.

If you must test your buoyancy in open water, be prepared to use your buoyancy compensator to re-establish positive buoyancy if you discover that you are grossly overweighted. Since each person has their own individual buoyancy and diving system it is impossible to predict here how much weight you will need to dive.

Most new dry suit divers have a tendency to use too much weight on their belts. This can cause serious problems in buoyancy control. A diver who uses an excess amount of weight must put a great deal of air in his suit to achieve neutral buoyancy. When this air shifts inside the suit, it can lead to buoyancy control problems for the untrained dry suit diver.

Your goal as a dry suit diver should be to dive with the minimum amount of weight possible and with the minimum volume of air inside your dry suit. You should wear only enough weight to allow you to make a 5 minute precautionary decompression stop at the end of your dive, at a depth of ten feet, when you have 500 P.S.I. of air remaining in your tank.

In Chapter 10 there is a complete discussion of zero gravity diving with a dry suit. It contains detailed information on how to achieve the proper trim underwater.

Chapter 9

Dressing Into Your Dry Suit System

Think back to the first time you dressed into a full 1/4 inch wetsuit. If you have been diving for a long time you probably don't remember how difficult it was to perform that simple task. However, once you learned some of the tricks involved in effectively dressing into your wetsuit it became much easier.

Learning to dress into a dry suit is not difficult, but there are definitely some techniques that will make doing so much simpler. With very little experience, you will probably find that dressing into a dry suit is much easier than dressing into a full 1/4 inch wetsuit!

Start Your Pre-Dive Check at Home

One of the most important tips to remember when using a dry suit is to check its condition before you leave for a dive trip. This check is especially important if you haven't used your suit recently. The pre-dive check should be performed several days before your trip to enable you to correct anything that might not be working properly. If you wait until the morning of your trip to discover that your neck seal has deteriorated you may not have the parts, or the time to properly repair it before the trip.

Start your pre-dive check with the zipper(s) on your dry suit. Open the zipper all the way. Carefully inspect all the teeth on the zipper to ensure that they are all present and that none of them are broken. Since the teeth are all symmetrically placed, any gaps in the teeth will immediately reveal that some are missing. You should not dive a suit that has a zipper with missing teeth. Missing teeth indicate a broken zipper. This condition could cause your suit to flood.

Leak test your dry suit if there is any possibility that it may have leaks.

Examine the zipper further by grasping it on one side with your hands a few inches apart. Gently bend the zipper in an arc, but do not force it to bend any further than it will go naturally. If you notice any spots where the zipper bends at a right angle this indicates that the tape that forms the base of the zipper is torn.

You should not dive a suit with a torn base tape. Damaged zippers can fail unexpectedly and cause your suit to flood. Frequent lubrication of the zipper will help prevent zipper damage.

To leak test your suit, twist rubber bands carefully, but tightly, around the wrist and neck seals to close the seals. Next, close the zipper. If your suit has an automatic exhaust valve, screw the adjustment all the way "closed". Attach the power inflator to your suit and inflate the suit until it is taut. Use a clean spray bottle and spray a dilute solution of soapy water on any suspected leaks. Leaking air will form bubbles on the suit and allow you to detect leaks quite easily.

The seals of your dry suit must be in good condition. Check the seals of your suit for nicks or tears. Neoprene seals can be repaired with wetsuit cement. Although you can dive them shortly after repairing them, it is best to wait over night before use. Always avoid temperatures over 100 degrees F with any new neoprene repairs. For wetsuit cement to fully cure it takes at least 10 days.

If your suit has latex seals, carefully examine them for signs of "checking" or cracking. Seals that are gummy or sticky are on the road to failure, too. If the seals are in poor condition they should be replaced before your dive. Latex seals that are weak may tear during normal dress-in routines.

Test the valves on your suit to ensure they are working correctly. Hook up your suit inflator and push the button several times. The button should not stick either open or closed. If you are unable to make your inflator valve work properly do not dive the suit until it is serviced. Salt crystals in the inflator mechanism are the most common cause of a stuck inflator button.

To test the exhaust valve you must seal your suit off with rubber bands like you would during a leak test. Inflate the suit until it is rigid and then operate the exhaust. Air should flow freely through the valve when it is activated and reseal completely.

In warm weather you'll want to set up as much equipment as possible before you dress into your dry suit.

Automatic exhaust valves should flow air freely when the suit is inflated fully. If the exhaust valve does not vent air properly check inside the suit for lint or other debris that may be blocking the valve. If there is no obvious obstruction it may be that the membrane in the valve has dried and stuck to the valve body. Try rinsing the valve and running water through it from the inside if possible. If you are still unable to get the exhaust valve to open or close normally do not use the suit until the valve has been serviced.

The importance of checking your suit several days before the dive can't be stressed enough, particularly if your suit has not been used for a few months. This is especially true if your latex seals are old, or you live in an area where there is smog. High ozone levels in smog will cause latex seals to deteriorate faster than usual.

The night before the dive it's a good idea to trim your fingernails if they are long. This will help prevent you from accidentally tearing a latex seal.

At the Dive Site

Topside weather at your dive site will affect your pre-dive procedures on the day of your dive. If the weather is cold or rainy, it may be more comfortable to dress into your dry suit before you set up your other equipment. If you are diving through ice, it may be safer to wear your dry suit on the surface than cold weather clothing and a life vest.

In warm weather you should set up all your other diving equipment before you dress into your dry suit. This means that your scuba system, weights, fins, mask and snorkel, and other accessories should be ready to go on the minute your dry suit zipper is closed. Most people find it very uncomfortable to stand around in a dry suit when the air temperature is warmer than 70 degrees F.

With certain types of dry gloves, such as those made for Viking and DUI by S.I. Tech, the cuff rings must be inserted into the dry suit sleeves before you dress into your suit. In fact, both the inner and outer rings should be installed in the suit when you set up the rest of your gear to dive. Some dry suit divers even install their cuff rings the night before the dive. Commercial divers sometimes install their cuff rings permanently, by gluing them to the suit, although this practice can make it difficult to clean silt or sand from underneath the outer ring.

Prior to dressing into your dry suit you should take the time to lubricate the seals. You may use either pure talcum powder or soapy water. Do not use silicone spray.

Talcum powder is a good lubricant in that it provides a dry, yet slippery surface. If talcum powder is used it must be pure talc, with no scent.

With certain types of dry gloves you may need to install the cuff rings before you dress into your dry suit.

Proper positioning of the outer cuff ring on a Viking suit.

Scented talc contains perfumes that are made from oils. The oil in the perfume can eat up latex and/or neoprene seals, causing them to deteriorate prematurely.

In warm weather, soapy water is also a good lubricant and makes donning your wrist seals even easier than with talc. Soapy water can be used to help you remove your wrist seals, too.

Silicone spray is not an acceptable lubricant for your dry suit seals. Although silicone spray will make it easy to dress in, it has a very negative effect when it is time to repair your suit. While some people claim that silicone spray will lengthen the life of your seals, we have seen no evidence of this.

When you apply silicone spray to your wrist and neck seals you will inevitably get some of the silicone onto the body of your suit. This silicone will impregnate the suit material. It can make it very difficult to get a good bond when it is time to apply new wrist or neck seals, even if you use solvent to "remove" the silicone. In the long run it is much easier and wiser not to use silicone spray, or any other commercially prepared "seal saver", on your suit or seals. Despite the recommendation of some dry suit manufacturers, we suggest that you do not use silicone spray on your dry suit's seals.

If you are using a polypropylene liner underneath your dry suit underwear you should don this layer completely before proceeding any further. Most people wear a bathing suit under their dry suit underwear, but you could wear a pair of shorts and a Tee shirt if you prefer. Whatever you find comfortable is acceptable.

Dressing into your dry suit underwear is much easier if you start by sitting down, especially if you are diving from a boat. Pull on the lower part of your underwear, then stand up to work your underwear over your hips.

Make sure you remove all of your jewelry before donning your dry suit.

Sit down to don the lower part of your dry suit underwear.

If you are diving from a large boat, and the deck is wet, make sure your underwear boots and dry suit are close at hand. It can be uncomfortable if you must walk across a wet, cold deck in your bare feet. If your dry suit underwear is open cell foam or pile, walking on a wet deck will leave your underwear boots wet and cold for the rest of the dive day. Once you have your underwear on it is time to get into your suit.

General Techniques for All Dry Suits

Stop! Before you do anything else make sure that you have removed your watch and any jewelry that may catch on a seal and cause it to tear. This includes ear rings, necklaces, rings, and bracelets. Anything that can tear a dry suit seal must be removed before you dress. More seals have been torn by divers getting dressed than have ever been damaged underwater.

When it is time to don your suit, it will be much safer and easier if you sit down to start the dress-in process. If your suit is equipped with suspenders make sure they are properly aligned before you step into the suit. They

If your suit is equipped with suspenders make sure they are properly aligned before you get into your suit.

Sit down to don the lower part of your dry suit.

should be pulled up and out to the side so they will be on the outside of your legs and body. Pull the suit onto your lower legs and get your feet firmly into the boots before you stand up.

Pull the dry suit up to your hips and waist. Depending upon the cut of your suit, women with broad hips may take a moment to get the suit past their buttocks. This is one of the places where a custom dry suit really pays off.

If your suit is equipped with suspenders you should slip them over your shoulders at this time. Adjust the tension on the suspenders so they are taut but not tight. They should be supporting the lower part of your suit. The suspenders themselves should still have stretch.

If your suit is not equipped with suspenders, just before you don the rest of your equipment, pull your suit up into your crotch as far as it will go. Close your legs and don your weight belt. This will make your suit more comfortable and it will not feel as though it is hanging down around your knees.

At this point, if your dry suit underwear is equipped with thumb tabs, slip the tabs over your thumbs. This will allow you to slide your arm down the sleeve without having your dry suit underwear bunch up at your forearm.

Some divers prefer to grab the thumb tabs between their fingers rather than slipping it over their thumbs. Whichever method you use be sure to release the thumb tabs once your hand is through the seals and tuck them back inside the suit so they don't cause your wrist seals to leak.

Insert either arm into the sleeve of your suit first. When your hand reaches the wrist seal, keep your fingers extended but squeeze them all together (including your thumb). This creates the smallest diameter for your hand to go through the wrist seal.

Grab the outside of the wrist seal with your free hand and gently pull it over the hand inside the suit. Grab the wrist seal itself; do not grab the sleeve of the suit. If you pull on the sleeve to get your hand through the seal you will place a strain on the suit where the seal mates to the suit. Take special care not to dig your fingernails into the seals. Only use your finger tips for donning all seals.

Another method that some divers use for getting their hand through the wrist seals is to slip two or three fingers of their free hand inside the opening of the wrist seal and pull the seal over the hand inside the sleeve. This technique also works well. Again, just be sure you don't dig your fingernails into the wrist seal.

If your seals are well lubricated you can insert both of your arms in the sleeves and try to pop both arms through the seals at one time. This method works well.

Once you have tucked the thumb tabs from your dry suit underwear back inside the suit, adjust your wrist seals. Most latex seals are designed to lay flat against your wrist. The seals should be as far up your arm as is required for them to seal effectively. There must be no underwear sticking out of the seal. Ideally there should be at least 1 inch of wrist seal material making direct contact with your wrists.

Slip the suspenders over your shoulders.

Neoprene wrist seals may either be cone shaped or designed to fold under. With a cone shaped seal, you need only check to make sure it is pushed far enough up your wrist to form an efficient seal.

Folding neoprene seals are tucked back underneath themselves. With this type of seal there should be a minimum of two inches of material folded under the top layer

The use of thumb tabs makes it easier to get the underwear properly installed in the dry suit sleeve.

The wrist seal should be as far up your arm as possible without causing discomfort.

Folding under a neoprene wrist seal.

photo by Kristine Barsky

This is the proper hand position for spreading a latex neck seal.

of neoprene. As with all other seals, there must be no underwear trapped under the seal to create a channel where water can leak in.

Once your wrist seals are properly adjusted, it's time to don your neck seal. The basic dress-in procedure is the same for most suits up to this point with the exception of the Unisuit. The Unisuit has a unique dress-in procedure where the neck seal is donned first, followed by the cone shaped wrist seals.

Donning Latex Neck Seals

To don a latex neck seal, reach through the neck seal with both hands, keeping your thumbs on the outside of the seal and suit. Spread the neck seal by pulling against the palms of your hands. Avoid any bunching of the seal since this makes it more difficult to get it over your head. Do not dig your fingers into the latex or you may cut the seal. Pull the neck seal gently, but firmly, over your head.

Divers with long hair may find it easier to don their neck seals if they wear an old nylon stocking over their head. Tuck your hair up into the stocking to get it out of the way. The nylon is quite slippery and helps to keep long hair from tangling in the seal. Some divers actually roll the nylon up onto their head like a cap, once they have the neck seal on. They leave the stocking in place when they dive so it is convenient to use again when they get out of the water.

Some latex neck seals are designed to folded under on themselves, similar to the manner in which a neoprene wrist seal is adjusted. Other latex seals are intended to be worn straight up. Whichever method the manufacturer of your suit recommends should be followed. However, regardless of the design, all latex seals should be worn as low on your neck as possible for maximum comfort.

Like any other seal, neck seals must be free of any interference that might interrupt the seal. Dry suit underwear collars and long hair can create leaks in neck seals if they are not properly adjusted. In addition, divers with long hair on the back of their neck may experience leakage due to hair interfering with the neck seal. If this is a problem you may want to have your hair dresser shave the back of your neck.

Donning Neoprene Neck Seals

Neoprene neck seals are also easy to don and adjust, although the procedure is slightly different from a latex seal. Although neoprene seals do not tear as easily as latex seals they can be damaged and take longer to repair. It's better to don your seal properly than to miss out on diving while you make a repair.

Pull the upper end of the dry suit of your head and position your head at the opening for the neck seal inside the suit. With your hands on the outside of the neck seal, use the friction of your hands on the neoprene to slide the seal over your head. Push your head up through the neck seal while pulling down with your hands.

Stop when the top edge of the neck seal reaches your chin. Grab the edge of the seal and turn it down and in on itself, just as you would a reverse turtleneck sweater, with the smooth "skin" side of the material against your neck.

General Instructions for All Waterproof Zippers

If you did not lubricate your dry suit zipper after you used your suit the last time, take the time to lubricate your zipper before you use it again. The extra minute it takes to lube the zipper will pay off in longer zipper life and smoother zipper action. Dry suit zippers are expensive and it's worth the effort to take good care of them.

Make sure the neck seal is properly adjusted on your neck.

If you have long hair, use an old nylon stocking to help get the neck seal over your head.

Donning a neoprene neck seal.

Adjusting a neoprene neck seal.

To properly lubricate the zipper, first close the zipper all the way. Use either paraffin wax of bee's wax, only. Keep in mind that cold surface temperatures will make it difficult to use paraffin wax. Do not use silicone spray or silicone grease on your dry suit zipper. If you use either of these lubricants they will work their way into the base material of the zipper tape. They can make it difficult or impossible to replace the zipper if necessary.

Lubricate the outside of the zipper only. Never lubricate the inside of the zipper. If you lubricate the inside of the zipper it will collect dirt and other debris that can cause the zipper to fail. It does not take a great deal of wax to lubricate the zipper. A thin film of wax is sufficient.

Always put your finger inside the loop on the zipper pull before you close the zipper. If you just hold onto the pull you can lose your grip and possibly hurt yourself or your dive buddy. Also, if you lose your grip this can cause the zipper to jerk, possibly causing you to accidentally jam underwear in the zipper.

Tuck all dry suit underwear out of the way to close the zipper. Pull the tab out and forward to close the zipper. Anything caught in the zipper will cause it to leak. In addition, any fabric caught in the zipper may damage it. If your zipper does jam on your underwear, work it very gently but firmly back away from the jam. Try not to force it.

Always ensure that the zipper slider is hard up against the stop. Even the slightest gap will cause the zipper to leak. Double check the zipper to make sure it is correctly closed. Your final tug should be firm, but smooth. Do not jerk the zipper!

Closing the Zipper On Self-Donning Suits

Pull the torso of the suit down and fasten the crotch strap first, if your suit is equipped with one. This will make it easier to close the self-don zipper. Put your finger in the loop on the zipper pull and close the zipper with a smooth action.

Your buddy should help you to close a back mounted zipper.

Closing the zipper on a self don suit.

After you have closed the dry suit zipper, close the outer protective zipper, if your suit is equipped with one. This outer zipper will help to prevent sand and other material from getting into the waterproof zipper.

Closing Back Mounted Zippers

For dry suits equipped with back mounted zippers, it is wise to have your buddy assist you in closing the zipper. While it's possible to attach a long string to the zipper pull, so you can close the zipper yourself, this is not a good idea. There is a strong possibility if you do this that you will catch your dry suit underwear in the zipper.

To close a back mounted zipper, lift your elbows to the height of your shoulders. Bring your arms forward until your elbows are just in front of your chest. This creates a gentle curve in the dry suit zipper that is the perfect angle for closing it.

If your dive buddy is not a dry suit diver, remind them to put their finger in the loop on the pull and tuck the underwear out of the way before they close the zipper. After the zipper is closed you should double check it to see that the slide is hard up against the stop.

Adjusting Dry Hoods

Dry hoods must be properly adjusted before you go in the water. Just as it is essential to make sure nothing interferes with a wrist seal or a neck seal, the same considerations hold true for using a dry hood. Remember, if you have a beard, a dry hood will not seal on it.

Latex dry hoods are designed to be used with a liner to provide insulation and give the hood shape. Never use a latex dry hood without the liner. It will not keep your head warm and the hood could seal over your ear causing a squeeze.

Note the warm neck collar just beneath the latex neck seal on this suit. The bib of your hood would be inserted between the two.

If you are using a latex dry hood, all of your hair and the liner must be tucked up underneath the hood.

Most of the hood liners are equipped with a chin strap that fastens onto the liner itself with Velcro®. Older liners did not have chin straps, but were equipped with Velcro tabs in the back of the suit. This arrangement did not work well. If your suit has these tabs you may want to remove them and purchase a liner with a chin strap. It is much more comfortable.

Fasten the chin strap securely under your chin and tuck your hair up inside the liner. Make sure the liner is centered on your head and not crooked. Next, grab the dry hood with both hands and stretch it up and over the liner. If the liner shifts forward or to the side you may need to reposition it.

Make sure the liner is not covering your forehead or that there are any stray hairs sticking out from under the dry hood. Your face mask is designed to seal over the hood. The bottom of the latex dry hood should be under your chin, unless you are using a full face mask. With a full face mask, the bottom of the dry hood should be covering your chin.

Adjusting Foam Neoprene Hoods

Some dry suits are designed with a special feature known as a "*warm neck collar*". This allows you to tuck the bib of a foam neoprene hood underneath a special collar so there is no gap between the bottom of the wetsuit hood and the neck seal on your dry suit. You will probably need some assistance to properly tuck the hood in underneath the warm neck collar in the back. The bib of the hood goes between the collar and the body of the suit.

Venting the Dry Suit

Once you have closed the zipper on your dry suit, you should vent your suit before you don any other equipment. This will make your suit more comfortable to wear on deck and will increase your safety when you enter the water. Entering the water from a height when your suit is full of air can cause your neck seal to vent air and leak.

To vent your suit, squat down, fold your arms across your chest, and manually open the exhaust valve. This will force the excess air out of your dry suit. You can also achieve the same effect by opening the neck seal with your fingers, but if you are not careful you can unknowingly get underwear trapped under the neck seal this way.

Have your buddy help you don your B.C.

When it is time to don your tank and buoyancy compensator, have your buddy assist you. Donning your B.C. by yourself when you are wearing a dry suit can be

Squat down and open the exhaust valve on your suit to get the air out of it before you go in the water.

difficult and there is a good chance you may damage your neck or wrist seals. Have your buddy hold your tank up or rest it on a bench as they steady it for you.

To don your B.C., loosen all of the strap adjustments to their widest opening. Insert your left arm first through the left B.C. shoulder strap, taking care that your dry suit exhaust valve clears the strap. Then insert your right arm through the right shoulder strap. If your arm catches on the strap do not force it through. Instead, allow your buddy to clear it and guide it through the harness. More than one dry suit diver has torn a wrist seal by forcing their arm past a B.C. strap.

After you have put on your tank and B.C. double check to make sure your weight belt has a clear drop path.

Test your dry suit inflator and exhaust valve before you enter the water.

Always take the time to test your dry suit inflator valve before you enter the water. Push the button several times to be sure it is operating freely and does not stick. It is better to discover a problem on the surface than to find out your valve is free flowing once you have started to descend.

Be sure to test the valves on your suit before you go in the water.

Chapter 10

Diving With Your Dry Suit System

Learning to dive with a dry suit is not difficult, but you will need to perfect a few new skills. Although this book is as comprehensive as possible, you should not attempt to dive a dry suit until you have completed a dry suit training course. This book is not a substitute for in-water training and experience. Take a complete dry suit training course from a certified instructor who is knowledgeable in dry suit diving techniques, before you dive your dry suit in open water without supervision.

Entering the Water

Entering the water in your dry suit is not much different from entering the water in your wetsuit. If you are diving from a large dive boat, be sure to get as much air out of your suit as possible before you make your entry. Vent the suit properly on deck before you hit the water.

Just before you jump in, if your suit has any excess material in the legs, reach down and pull it up above your knee. This will allow you to bend your legs easier when you are in the water and will reduce the air volume in the lower legs of the suit.

photo © 1991 by John Heine

Make sure you vent most of the air from your dry suit before you hit the water.

109

To properly vent an automatic exhaust valve, lift your left arm until the valve is at the highest point.

To assure yourself of being buoyant after your entry, add just enough air to your buoyancy compensator to allow yourself to float. A couple of puffs of air should be all you need if you are properly weighted.

The first thing you will notice after you enter the water is that when you are upright (vertical) on the surface, there will be more pressure on your feet than on your chest. This is due to the pressure differential caused by the water over the length of your body. Air migrates inside the suit to the highest point on your body.

This phenomenon is known as an *"underpressure"*, and is common to all dry suits. If you turned upside down in your dry suit you would experience an underpressure on your chest. Technically speaking, an underpressure is a form of squeeze, but proper dry suit underwear, and the use of the suit inflator as you descend, will prevent any injury.

Whenever you enter the water with your dry suit always take a moment to check the system for leaks. Concentrate to determine if your suit is taking on water at any point. If your suit is leaking, for any reason, take the time to get out of the water to correct the problem. A small leak on the surface may not always get worse underwater, but it will continue throughout your dive. You will be very wet if the problem is not fixed and you continue to dive. Do not dive if your suit is leaking.

Checking Buoyancy (Getting Neutral)

Testing that your're neutral in your dry suit is almost identical to testing for buoyancy in your wetsuit. The principles are all the same; you just have to deal with the additional volume of air in the dry suit.

First, put your regulator in your mouth and breathe normally. Vent all the air out of your buoyancy compensator. You should still be floating at this point.

Next, vent all the air out of your dry suit. In reality, although we say "vent all the air out of your suit", there will always be some air left inside your dry suit.

If you have a manual exhaust, raise the valve to the highest point possible and push the button. If the valve is mounted on your chest, lean back in the water so the valve is on or near the surface.

If you have an automatic exhaust valve it will probably be mounted on your left arm. Lift your left elbow out of the water, but keep your arm bent and your hand pointed towards the bottom. Open the exhaust valve all the way, usually by turning the valve counterclockwise. Even if you are unable to see the valve, due to your equipment, you should be able to hear air hissing out of the valve and feel it bubbling. When all the air is out of the suit, you still should not sink at this time.

Take a deep breath, fill your lungs, and do not exhale. Hang motionless in the water in a vertical position with your head up. If you are properly weighted, or _neutral,_ you should be floating with your eyes at the water level. If you are sinking at this time you are heavy, or _negative._ If you are floating higher than eye level you are too _buoyant._

While you are still vertical in the water, exhale all the air in your lungs. You should start to sink very slowly. If you do not sink, you are too buoyant. If you sink rapidly you are too negative. Add or subtract weights as needed. Now you are weighted for being neutral, but you have not finished your buoyancy adjustment. You must still make adjustments for your precautionary decompression stop.

For your first dry suit dive, add 2/3 the weight of the buoyancy change of your scuba cylinder from full to empty. For example, if your tank experiences a 6 pound shift to positive buoyancy as it empties, add 4 additional pounds of weight to your belt. You will probably need to adjust this weight by a little bit either way, but this is a good place to start.

Try this on your first dive, and make your ascent at the end of your dive next to a weighted line. See if you are able to make the necessary precautionary decompression stop. If you find yourself too buoyant at 15 feet with 500 P.S.I. of air in your tank, be prepared to stop your ascent by holding onto the weighted line. You should still be capable of becoming neutral at a depth of 10 feet when it is time for you to exit the water. Add or subtract weight on your next dive to fine tune your buoyancy. Remember, your goal is to dive with the minimum amount of weight possible and the minimum volume of air inside your dry suit.

Proper Descent Technique

To start your dive, vent all the air out of your buoyancy compensator. Next, vent the air out of your dry suit by using the exhaust valve. If you have an automatic exhaust valve, open it all the way and leave it open

Add air to your dry suit in short bursts as you descend.

Use a lift bag to raise heavy objects underwater. Never use your dry suit for lifting.

throughout your dive. Exhale the air from your lungs and you should slowly start to sink, feet first.

After you have sunk a few feet you will notice that you will start to descend even faster. Why? Because even though you got "all the air" out of your dry suit, the remaining air inside the suit has started to compress. As you continue to descend, your body will naturally rotate to a more horizontal position and eventually most people turn head down. This will allow you to observe the bottom below you more completely.

As you begin to feel the "squeeze" on your body, push the inflator button on your suit to add enough air inside the suit to relieve the pressure, use only short bursts. Add just enough air to relieve suit squeeze and control your descent. You should be able to stop your descent at any time by adding just enough air to make yourself neutral at that depth.

Proper Dry Suit Trim Underwater

Once you reach the bottom, adjust your buoyancy using only your dry suit so that you are neutral. Do not add air to your buoyancy compensator to adjust your buoyancy. It is very difficult to control your buoyancy when you have air in two separate compartments at the same time, i.e., the B.C. and your suit. Controlling both air compartments is an advanced dry suit diving skill and is not recommended for the novice dry suit diver.

If you pick up additional weight during your dive, such as abalone or lobster, consider using a small lift bag attached to your goody bag to raise the bag. This is much safer than trying to use your buoyancy compensator to lift this weight. The danger of using your B.C. is that if you lose control of the object you will suddenly have a great deal of excess positive buoyancy. This can cause an uncontrolled ascent leading to decompression sickness or air embolism.

To raise heavy objects, like a porthole or anchor, use a large lift bag. Do not attempt to raise heavy objects using your dry suit and/or B.C.

Underwater your dry suit should feel as though it is gripping you gently, but firmly all over your body. This will feel unusual at first, but will be less noticeable as you make more dives with your suit. The sensation is quite different from wearing a wetsuit. However, there should be no discomfort from the suit.

There should not be a large bubble of air inside your suit, nor should you notice massive air shifts if you change position in the water. There should only be a minimum volume of air inside the suit.

Zero Gravity Diving

Few things in diving give as much pleasure as being suspended in midwater with complete neutral trim. The ability to hover at any depth in complete comfort will improve your diving whether you are an underwater photographer, wreck diver, hunter, or explorer. We call this experience *zero gravity diving* or *zero G diving*.

Zero G diving has two major components. First, the diver is neutral. He does not drift up or down. Secondly, the diver is properly trimmed. Both his head and feet are at the same depth, and he does not list to one side or the other. This is the most efficient position for swimming.

Each diver's adjustment to zero G diving with a dry suit will be somewhat different. The actions you take depends upon your body size and structure, the type of dry suit you use, the amount of dry suit underwear you wear, the amount of weight you need, the type of cylinder you use, and any other pieces of equipment you take with you when you dive.

To determine how you are trimmed, imagine a line drawn through the center of your body, running from your head to your toes. In an ideal situation as you swim underwater this line should be parallel to the bottom. This posture creates the least amount of drag.

In reality, most open water divers swim in a slightly head up position so they can keep an eye on where they are going. Many cave divers and wreck divers swim in a slightly head down position to avoid stirring up silt with their fins. If we wanted to get technical, we could measure your swimming attitude in degrees from the horizontal.

You will increase the drag on your body as you assume a head's up, or head's down, position. This happens because you have increased the amount of surface area you present to the water. As you increase your drag, you must work harder. This leads to increased air consumption and can also lead to exhaustion.

Your trim can also be affected by the amount of "roll" we experience from side to side. If you have more weight on one side of your weight belt than another, or if you mount a pony bottle on one side of your primary scuba cylinder, this will cause you to roll or list to one side.

Prototype model of DUI's Weight and Trim system.

The two factors that have the greatest effect on your trim are your center of gravity and your center of buoyancy. Your center of gravity is the area where your body mass is concentrated. When you add a scuba tank and weights this changes somewhat, but generally it will still be near your stomach.

If most of your weights are towards your back and you are wearing a negative cylinder, this mass will have a tendency to roll you onto your back. This will be especially true if you wear a buoyancy compensator that puts most of the buoyancy in front of you. In most cases, this combination of equipment will produce a head's up swimming attitude.

The location of your center of buoyancy will be determined by your personal buoyancy, your dry suit, your buoyancy compensator, and any other equipment worn. As the air shifts position when your body moves through the water, the location of your center of buoyancy can change dramatically.

When your center of gravity and center of buoyancy are in exactly the same position it is possible to rotate to any position, but you may need to work hard to stay in that position. The ideal situation is to position your center of buoyancy directly _over_ your center of gravity. This makes you extremely stable underwater with no tendency to roll.

Weight belts place your "ballast" in the small of your back, a location that places a great deal of stress on your spine. Your spine is much better at carrying a load when your body is in a vertical position, but this is impractical for swimming. By changing the position of your weights and shifting the load onto your shoulders you relieve much of the stress caused by your weight belt and improve your swimming attitude through the water. Keep in mind that the only way to determine your personal center of gravity and center of buoyancy is to experiment in the water.

Weighting systems such as DUI's Weight and Trim system allow you to shift your weights forward or backward on the belt and to adjust the weights up or down on your body. This system is intended to be used by divers with advanced diving skills who have been specially trained to adjust their trim underwater.

Dry Suit Leaks

photo © 1991 by Bob Cranston

It is not uncommon during the course of a dive to sometimes get a little bit of water inside your dry suit, even if your suit is working perfectly. The usual points of entry are at the wrist seals and the neck seal.

Some divers have very pronounced tendons at their wrists. If you flex your wrist underwater, to operate a camera or other piece of equipment, this can create a channel for water to enter your dry suit. Normally this should be no more than perhaps a tablespoon of water. This is a

If you are new to dry suit diving, have your instructor check your suit to make sure you have adjusted all of the seals properly.

very normal event and almost all divers will experience this from time to time. This effect can be reduced by pushing the seal above the exposed tendons.

Any seal that is not adjusted properly will leak, too. This can occur when underwear or hair is trapped under a seal. When a seal is pinched or twisted it will almost always leak.

Another cause of an occasional leak is through the neck seal. If you twist your neck at an unusual angle the tendons on your neck can also contribute to water leakage. Again, most divers will have this happen to them occasionally.

The most common dry suit leaks are from a zipper that has not been closed completely. Punctures can also occur if an inflator valve stem is jammed against the suit during transport. The sharp edge of the stem can cut through any dry suit materials and create a leak.

While it is rare to tear a dry suit, pinhole punctures are the most common source of leakage and damage. Sea urchins in particular can go through almost any dry suit. Sharp pieces of metal on ship wrecks will penetrate most dry suits with ease.

Venting air from an automatic exhaust valve.

You can also use the manual override to vent air from some automatic exhaust valves.

For extra protection, serious wreck divers will sometimes wear a pair of cotton coveralls over their dry suits. This is acceptable as long as the coveralls do not interfere with the operation of the valves on your suit. Also, be aware that the coveralls will add weight and drag to your diving system and may interfere with your swimming.

Ascending in Your Dry Suit

When you are ready to ascend, if you have an automatic exhaust valve, check to be sure that the valve is open all the way before you begin your ascent. Raise your left upper arm so that the valve is as high (shallow) as possible in relation to the rest of your body, and ascend slowly. Do not extend your hand above your arm since this will trap air above the valve, between the valve and your wrist, where it cannot vent. If you are using a push to dump valve, raise your arm so the valve is at the highest point and push in on the valve with your other hand.

Your first few ascents and descents should be conducted next to a weighted line to allow you to stop your descent if you need to do so. If you have a manual valve you should keep one hand on the valve at all times during your ascent and vent air as needed. Air does not vent through a dry suit as fast as it does through a buoyancy compensator. The air must travel through the underwear to escape through the valve. Some of the more "earthy" divers we know refer to venting air through your dry suit exhaust valve as *"passing gas"*.

If you are using an automatic exhaust valve and find yourself ascending faster than you should, lift your upper arm higher and the valve will vent faster. If the valve is still not venting enough air, push down on the top of the valve with your right hand to vent the valve manually. Keep in mind that some valves actually dump *slower* when manually depressed since you are compressing the valve against the underwear which may block the valve. You may also want to stop your ascent by holding on to the line until you can vent off any excess air.

You can also slow your ascent by using your fins. By holding your ankles rigid with your fins parallel to the surface you can slow your ascent dramatically. The fins act as "dive brakes". To maximize this effect, arch your back and hold your arms out parallel to the surface, too. This technique is known as *"flaring"*. Flaring will slow a rapid ascent, but it will not stop it completely. Another technique used is to swim horizontally, so your body presents a greater surface area, to slow your ascent.

As you get closer to the surface, exhaust more air from your suit, particularly as you near 20 feet. Remember that most dive computers call for slower rates of ascent the nearer you get to the surface. Watch your depth gauge/dive computer carefully so you do not overshoot your precautionary decompression stop.

Once you have reached the surface, immediately inflate your buoyancy compensator just enough to give yourself buoyancy. It is far more comfortable to snorkel back to the boat this way than by making yourself buoyant by infalating your dry suit. If you put enough air in your dry suit to give yourself buoyancy you will create uncomfortable pressure on your neck seal from air in the dry suit and find awkward to move around on the surface.

Exiting the Water

If you are diving from an inflatable boat you will probably want to remove your weight and cylinder before you try to climb back aboard. Re-

Use your buoyancy compensator for establishing buoyancy at the surface for snorkeling.

Keep an eye on your depth gauge or dive computer as you ascend so you can be sure to make a precautionary decompression stop at 10 feet at the end of your dive.

move your weight belt first and hand this up. If you must leave your weight belt on, be sure your exhaust valve is closed and there is enough air in your suit to provide you with positive buoyancy after you have removed your tank and B.C. Disconnect the inflator from your suit, remove your tank and B.C., and hand your tank into the boat.

Diving from a large boat is usually a bit easier when it is time to exit the water. On some charter boats, the crew members will actually help you to remove your fins once you are back on the swim step. Once you are back on deck, disconnect your power inflator and have your buddy help you remove your cylinder.

Beach diving in a dry suit requires more care than other dive locations, particularly if you are diving from a sandy beach. Be especially careful to avoid getting sand in your dry suit zipper and valves. If at all possible, don't remove your suit until you are standing on a clean towel or paved parking lot.

Disconnect your suit inflator hose if the valve sticks open.

Dry Suit Diving Emergency Techniques

Modern dry suits are very reliable, but you should always be prepared for the unexpected to happen underwater. During your dry suit training course, your instructor should show you how to deal with any potential problem that might arise when using a dry suit. Although these incidents are rare, you will be able to dive with greater confidence knowing that you are prepared to handle these emergencies. To maintain proficiency, you must practice your emergency skills on a regular basis under controlled conditions. We recommend that you practice your emergency skills frequently.

If you do not properly maintain your dry suit, one of the situations you may encounter is an inflator valve that sticks open. If this happens, your suit will inflate continuously.

The first thing you should attempt to do if your inflator valve sticks open is to disconnect your inflator hose immediately, and vent excess air through the exhaust valve at the same time. You will only be able to do both actions simultaneously if your suit is equipped with an automatic exhaust valve. If your suit has a manual exhaust and you must choose one action over the other, disconnect the suit inflator hose first. Then vent the manual exhaust.If

Be prepared to vent air from your wrist seals or neck seal if you are unable to vent enough air through the exhaust valve.

you are unable to disconnect the power inflator, but manage to control your buoyancy by using the exhaust valve, stop and get control of the situation before you ascend. Although some dry suit exhaust valves are purported to vent air faster than their accompanying inflator can supply it, certain underwear, suit, and harness combinations will inhibit this from happening.

Even if you are able to control the suit with a stuck power inflator while you are submerged, you may be unable to maintain control during your ascent. In any case, you should be prepared to vent air by opening either your wrist seal or neck seal during your ascent. Of course, you will get wet if you are forced to take this action.

Some older styles of pile underwear produced balls of lint when the suit rubbed against the underwear. When an exhaust valve gets clogged with lint it may be blocked to the point that it will not exhaust air properly. If the valve jams open, your suit will not properly hold air and you will probably get wet. You will be able to trap some air above the valve, in the neck and shoulders of the suit, particularly if you keep your right shoulder high. In this situation you should abort your dive and get out of the water.

Should your exhaust valve become clogged with lint, you probably won't notice this until it is time to ascend. If you notice that your exhaust valve is not operating properly you should immediately stop your ascent, if possible. If your suit is equipped with an automatic exhaust valve, try rotating the valve or operating it manually. If your suit is equipped with a manual exhaust there will probably be little you can do to get it to work if it is clogged.

Exhaust valves can also become jammed if the valve has not been properly maintained. Any contaminants that have dried in the valve, could effectively seal the rubber flapper in the valve to the valve body. This would prevent the valve from flowing air.

It is easy to right yourself from an upside down position if you have been properly trained.

In the event your valve will not exhaust properly, try to make your ascent on the anchor line, on a kelp stalk, or by following the bottom contour if possible. Stop and vent your suit through the cuff or neck seal every few feet. As long as your air supply will hold out, it is better to get a little wet than to violate your ascent rate and possibly suffer from decompression sickness, or air embolism.

If you must ascend in mid-water, with nothing to slow your ascent, be prepared to vent your suit rapidly through the wrist or neck if need be. Yet while you must be able to vent rapidly, you also need to control your ascent so that you don't lose so much buoyancy you start to sink again.

Loosing your weight belt underwater while wearing a dry suit will result in becoming very buoyant with an extremely rapid ascent. In this situation it is doubtful you will be able to vent enough air through the exhaust valve to get control of this predicament. Work to stop your ascent and be prepared to vent air from your suit from the wrist seal or neck seal.

Rather than lose your weight belt you should try to maintain an awareness of what is happening with your gear at all times while you are underwater. The experienced diver can concentrate on his or her dive, yet immediately knows when any piece of equipment is not acting right. Learn to develop this awareness. You should instantly know when your belt is loose or has slid off center from your waist.

Most divers who experience buoyancy problems with dry suits encounter this difficulty because they have worn too much weight. Too much weight on your belt forces you to add a large volume of air to your suit. When this air shifts it can cause problems for the untrained dry suit diver.

A properly trained and properly weighted dry suit diver has no problem in assuming any position they want to in the water. As long as you have a minimum volume of air inside your suit it is possible to turn upside down or do somersaults underwater without difficulty. However, if you are wearing excess weight, and have a high volume of air in your suit, righting yourself from an upside down position can be tough to do.

If you are upside down and have excess air in the feet of your dry suit, it can be difficult to regain an upright position. If your suit is not equipped with ankle straps it can cause your fins to pop off.

Righting yourself from an upside down position is usually not too difficult if you are not excessively buoyant. Ordinarily, all you need to do is tuck your body into a ball, give a slight kick, and roll to an upright position. Once you are right side up immediately vent your suit through the exhaust valve to regain control.

In the event of a catastrophic dry suit failure you may need to ditch your weight belt. If you can return to the surface with the buoyancy in your B.C. do this first, then drop the belt.

If your dry suit is completely flooded, even if you ditch all your weights you may still be negative.

If you are upside down and find yourself floating off the bottom, kick hard towards the bottom, bend at the waist, and push off the bottom to achieve a heads up position. Push in whichever direction will help you turn right side up. Again, vent your suit right away to get control of your buoyancy.

In a worst case scenario, if you are upside down, unable to right yourself, and headed toward the surface, all you can do is flare out in that position. You will undoubtedly exceed the ascent rate required by the dive tables and/or your dive computer. Be sure that you are exhaling in this situation to avoid a lung over-pressure injury.

Keep in mind that as most dry suit underwear gets wet, it becomes less buoyant. A little bit of water won't make much difference. However, if you completely flood your suit, you may need to either ditch your weights, or add air to your B.C., to maintain positive buoyancy at the surface.

Only in extremely rare cases does a dry suit ever flood completely. We refer to this as a catastrophic dry suit failure. These cases might occur with

If your dry suit zipper or neck seal fails, you can end up with quite a bit of water in your suit. Diving instructor John Heine demonstrates just how much water a flooded suit can hold. Note the bulging legs of this suit.

the complete failure of a zipper, blow-out of a neck seal, or the destruction of a valve. If you get a little bit of water inside your suit (and everyone does occasionally) that is <u>not</u> a flood. On the other hand, if your suit is completely full of water, and will not hold air properly, that is a serious situation.

Should your dry suit become full of water, depending upon the type of suit and underwear you are wearing, you will probably become negative. In most cases, depending upon the volume of your buoyancy compensator, you can return to the surface by inflating your B.C. Even in a completely flooded dry suit, with the zipper fully open, you can usually trap some air in the upper part of the suit (unless the neck seal has failed). This will be enough to give you slight positive buoyancy if you have ditched your weight belt.

With some dry suit/underwear combinations, if the suit is completely flooded, you will not become positively buoyant even if you drop your weight belt. You will probably be able to swim to the surface under your own power, but you should be prepared to use your B.C. in this situation if you find yourself still negative.

One of the most dangerous aspects of a flooded dry suit is that a suit in these circumstances will hold a great deal of water. The weight of the water inside the suit can make it very difficult to exit the water whether you are diving from the beach or from a boat. It may be necessary for your buddy to carefully make a small hole with his knife in each of the legs of your suit to drain the water out before you attempt to climb a ladder or stand up.

Opening the Zipper After the Dive

While you are out of the water, between dives, you may want to open up your dry suit to avoid overheating. This will generally be true for most people any time the air is warmer than 65 degrees F. Some divers may ac-

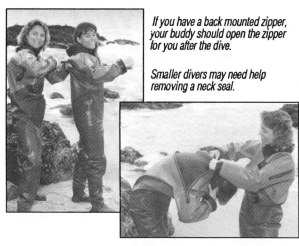

If you have a back mounted zipper, your buddy should open the zipper for you after the dive.

Smaller divers may need help removing a neck seal.

tually want to remove their entire dry suit, or at least peel down the upper portion. You may also need to remove at least part of the suit to use the toilet.

If your suit is equipped with a back mounted zipper, have your buddy open the zipper for you. Be sure to remind them to put their finger in the loop on the zipper pull. If you are wearing an older Unisuit or a Parkway Thermopro II, you can start the zipper, but your buddy will need to unzip the back for you.

If you are wearing a suit with cross chest zipper, it's a simple matter to unzip the suit yourself. If that action does not provide sufficient cooling you may want to get out of the top portion of the suit.

Removing a Latex Neck Seal

For divers with cross chest zippers on self donning dry suits, it's best to release the crotch strap on your suit and pull the torso up before you remove your neck seal. Get the suit as high on your body as possible before you remove the neck seal.

With your fingernails against your neck, slide the fingers of each hand down between the neck seal and your neck. Keep your thumbs on the outside of the neck seal. Grasp the neck seal firmly with both hands, but make sure you are only grabbing the neck seal, that you don't have a handful of underwear, too. Spread the neck seal by pulling it against the palms of your hands. Tuck your chin to your chest and lift up with your arms. The neck seal should slide over your head easily.

Smaller divers may need assistance getting the neck seal over their head. Your buddy can help you with this. Have your buddy grab the suit at the zipper, on the side of the zipper closest to your head. Have them lift the zipper gently over your head. They must understand that they cannot pull hard on the zipper or put a strain on it. They should only be _lifting_ the zipper. If they pull hard on the zipper this can cause the tape to tear.

Removing Latex Wrist Seals

Insert the first two fingers of your left hand under the wrist seal on the right sleeve of your suit, with your **fingernails against your wrist**. Slide your fingers down inside the sleeve until they are past the wrist seal. Take extra care not to catch your fingernails on the wrist seal.

Grasp the sleeve of the suit just above the wrist seal by holding it between your thumb and fingers. Pull your right hand through the wrist seal and inside the sleeve. Pull your arm out of the sleeve and repeat the operation for the other wrist seal.

An application of soapy water to your wrist can make it easier to remove a wrist seal, particularly if your suit is equipped with the heavy duty seals used on commercial suits. Sometimes it is easier to remove heavy duty seals with the aid of a buddy. Have them slide their thumbs in on either side of the wrist seal and grab the sleeve of the suit between their thumbs and fingers. They can then spread the seal and slide it over your wrist.

Divers with shoulder mounted zippers may be tempted to turn a sleeve inside out to aid them in removing a wrist seal. Don't do it! This action places a heavy strain on the docking end of the zipper and could break it.

Removing a Neoprene Neck Seal

Unroll the neck seal so it is no longer turned under on itself. Grab the neck seal with both hands, with your fingers inside and your thumbs on the outside. Do not dig your fingernails into the seal. Pull the neck seal up until the leading edge of the seal is at your chin and as high on the back of your head as you can.

The edge of the seal should be in the joint between your thumb and forefinger. Grasp the seal firmly, tuck your chin, and pull the seal up and over your head.

Removing Neoprene Wrist Seals

To remove a fold-under neoprene wrist seal, start by pulling the seal of your suit up your arm to allow them to invert. Turn the seal so that the nylon lays flat against your forearm. Insert the fingers of your opposite hand into the sleeve. Grab the sleeve just above the point where the wrist seal meets the sleeve. Pull the sleeve off your arm. To remove a cone-shaped neoprene seal, have your buddy put their thumbs inside the seal, spread it, and pull it over your wrist.

Removing a Unisuit

Getting out of an older Unisuit or Parkway Thermopro II is different from any other dry suit. You must take your time and be patient.

With the zipper all the way open, spread the rear opening of the suit and sit down. Make sure you are not sitting on the zipper. Put your left foot on your right knee and pull your left leg out of the suit. You may need to stretch the suit to do this, but don't pull on the zipper. Put your right foot on your left knee and remove this leg from the suit. You can then remove the wrist seals and neck seal, in that order.

Between Dives

A suit equipped with suspenders will stay in position between dives, even if you have peeled the top down, while you walk around topside. For a loose fitting dry suit without suspenders, you may want to tie the arms in a knot, or tuck the arms inside the dry suit (only if they are dry). If this action is not taken your suit will gradually slide down your body, making it difficult to walk. You can also use a weight belt without weights or a bungee cord around your waist to hold the suit in position. If you use a bungee cord make sure the ends of the hook are wrapped with tape to prevent them from cutting your suit or seals.

Wet or damp dry suit underwear should be dried between dives. Open cell foam underwear should be wrung out, particularly if it is very wet, before you put it in a drier.

Wooly bears and other types of underwear may also be wrung out. If no drier is available you can also try twirling the underwear in a circle over your head to spin the water out using centrifugal force. If the weather is warm enough, the underwear can be dried by hanging it on a hanger although this can take quite some time depending upon the type of underwear. Some dive boats have driers on them that you can use for this purpose. Remember, if your underwear contains Thinsulate®, do not use high heat for drying.

Larger ships may have blower systems to vent engine room air. Hanging your underwear in front of a blower vent will allow it to dry quickly. Be sure to carry a dry bag to stow your underwear when you aren't wearing it and to keep it dry for the trip home.

If the inside of your suit is wet, turn the suit inside out and allow it to dry, too. This is especially important with suits with a cotton lining that may take quite a while to dry.

You may want to peel down the top part of your suit between dives.

photo by Kristine Barsky

Keeping Cool Between Dives

On warm days it can get very hot inside a dry suit. If you must keep your suit on between dives you should take care not to overheat. There are several techniques that can be used to solve this problem. The simplest solution is to remove all of your other diving equipment except your fins and stay wet.

Other cooling methods to be considered are keeping your hands in a tub of ice water, or flowing cold water over your head and suit. A wet towel wrapped around the head can also be effective. Periodically dunk the towel in cold water and reapply it as needed. Always take care not to overheat.

Dry suit diving is fun!

photo by Ronnie Damico

Chapter 11

Maintenance of Your Dry Suit System

Dry suits require a bit more maintenance than wet suits. No one will deny that fact. However, that little bit of extra maintenance is well worth it when you hit the water knowing you will be warm and your suit is in top condition. The few minutes required to properly maintain your dry suit will pay off in fewer repairs and a longer lasting suit.

Checking Your Suit After the Dive

Once you are out of the water, after your dive, as a matter of routine you should check your dry suit when you first open the zipper. If your dry suit underwear feels or looks wet, look for possible points of water entry.

Most "leaks" are the result of an improperly adjusted seal or a channel created by the tendons in your wrist or hair at your neck. A damp underwear cuff or water around the collar of your underwear is a good clue that water entered at those points. Wet spots on your stomach or legs may indicate a puncture. Water on your left arm may indicate a leaking exhaust valve.

Take the time to examine your suit while you are still wearing it if you suspect your suit is damaged. This action will save you time later when you must locate the damage to make the repair.

After you have removed your suit, feel down inside the bottom of the suit, all the way down to the boots. Even if your suit didn't leak, the inside of your suit may still be damp due to condensation from your sweat.

On a warm day, most people will sweat a bit inside their dry suit and may never realize it. Although the upper body of your suit may be dry, the

Rinse your dry suit thoroughly after diving.

Periodically, wash the seals of your suit with soap and water.

sweat from your body will usually accumulate on the walls of your suit and then drain into the boots and lower legs. If this is the case, you will probably want to rinse the inside of your suit when you get home to prevent any mold or mildew from growing inside your suit. Check your suit after the dive and check it again when you get home.

Rinsing Your Suit After Diving

When it is time to rinse your suit after diving be sure to do a thorough job, especially if you have been diving in salt water or there is sand on your suit. Dry suit valves and zippers must be thoroughly rinsed after ocean diving.

Close the wrist seal and neck seal of your suit with rubber bands to prevent water entry while rinsing your suit (unless your suit is already wet inside). Close the zipper on your suit, too. Rinse the exterior of the suit completely, paying particular attention to the valves and zippers. Rinse the zipper thoroughly. Run water over it to help remove any sand or grit that you may have picked up on your suit during the dive.

Operate the valves as you run water over them. If your suit has an automatic exhaust valve, rotate the head of the valve as you run water through it. Push the inflator button several times as you run water over the outside of the mechanism.

It isn't possible to run fresh water directly through most inflator valves. To get water through the valve you need to flow water in the inlet and hook up your inflator hose. Depress the valve button and allow the water in the nipple to spray inside the suit. You can also lubricate the valve with a small amount of pump silicone liquid this same way. Dried salt crystals and corrosion inside an inflator valve are a major cause of stuck inflator buttons. Be sure that there is no salt remaining between the valve button and the valve body.

If your suit is wet or damp inside you should rinse the inside of the suit, too. Run fresh water inside the suit and drain it out several times. This is especially important if you have a suit with a cotton lining, such as a Viking or a Nokia.

Latex seals should be periodically washed with mild soap and water. This procedure will help to remove body oils that will destroy the seals prematurely.

Cleaning the Zipper

Dry suit zippers need special attention if you want to get the most life from them. They should receive an extra cleaning at least once a year, or more frequently if you dive often.

To clean a dry suit zipper, use a mild soap solution (such as Ivory) and an old toothbrush. Scrub the zipper teeth vigorously, inside and outside with the toothbrush. This will help to remove corrosion from the zipper and allow it to slide more easily. Brush between the teeth to remove old wax and grit.

Dry suit zippers should be cleaned vigorously using a toothbrush

Proper Drying

Your dry suit should be hung over a line, *out of the sun,* where it will receive good air circulation. Vulcanized rubber dry suits, TLS suits, and pack cloth suits will dry very quickly on the outside, but other types of dry suits may take some time for the exterior to dry. If your suit is equipped with ankle straps or suspenders hang it from these devices. This

Turn your suit inside out to allow the inside of the suit to dry.

will help the inside to dry more quickly than if you drape the entire suit over a line or rod.

After the outside of your suit is dry, carefully turn it inside out. Avoid stressing the docking ends of the dry suit zipper when you do this. Allow the inside of your suit to dry thoroughly. Suits with nylon knit linings may take several hours to dry thoroughly.

Check your suit when you think the inside is dry. Pay particular attention to the inside of the boots. These are hard to turn inside out on most suits and water may be trapped in them if you are unable to completely expose them.

When your suit is completely dry, both inside and outside, turn it right side out again. Take extra care with the zipper as you do this.

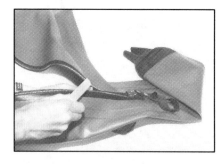

Zippers should be lubricated with paraffin wax or bee's wax.

Zipper Lubrication

Your dry suit zipper may be lubricated with either bee's wax or paraffin wax. These are the only two acceptable lubricants. Never use silicone spray or grease on your dry suit zipper.

Any excess paraffin wax should be removed from your dry suit after lubricating the zipper. Paraffin wax will cause deterioration of latex seals if left in contact with the seal for long periods of time.

Proper Storage

As we've mentioned before, never apply silicone spray to the seals of your dry suit. This will not help extend the life of your seals and makes repairs more difficult.

Inspect your suit before you put it away. Look at the seals and stretch them to detect signs of aging or cracking.

Your dry suit should be rolled for storage with the zipper left either open or closed, depending upon your manufacturer's recommendation. Some people feel there is less stress on the zipper when it is left open. They believe it is less prone to breakage if the suit is dropped, or if anything heavy (like a weight belt) is dropped on the zipper.

Some manufacturers recommend that you roll your suit up with the suit lying on its front, while others recommend that the suit be on its back. Again, follow the recommendations for your suit. The important point is that you roll the suit and cap your inflator valve if it is has a metal stem that may contact the suit. Inflator valve stems can puncture a dry suit if they are not capped before you roll your suit for storage. If you roll your suit with the inflator valve on the outside you will not puncture your suit with the valve stem.

After you have rolled up the body of the suit, fold the arms of the suit over the body. Place your suit in its storage bag. If no bag was provided with your suit, put it inside a plastic trash bag and seal it up.

Store your suit in a bag for maximum suit life.

The goal of proper storage is to prevent ozone and sunlight from damaging your suit. This will extend the life of latex seals greatly, especially if you live in a smoggy environment such as southern California. If the bag provided with your suit does not seal well you may want to place the suit and bag inside a plastic trash bag anyway.

Store your suit in a cool, dry place, away from electric motors or gas hot water heaters. Both electric motors and gas hot water heaters produce ozone, a chemical that will attack all rubber and latex seals. Oxygen and U.V. light are also detrimental to suit seals.

Laundering Dry Suit Underwear

Don't forget to take care of your dry suit underwear, too. Follow the manufacturer's directions for laundering.

Chapter 12

Dry Suit Repairs

Repairing a dry suit is no more complicated than repairing a wetsuit. The techniques are very similar, but they just aren't as widely known. The most important elements of dry suit repair are to have all of the correct repair materials, to take your time, and to be patient.

Locating Punctures

Punctures are the most common type of damage that most dry suits sustain. Punctures that usually occur while diving are from sea urchins or other sharp objects. Even a small puncture can leave you wet. However, a puncture would rarely, if ever, cause your suit to flood completely.

Locating the puncture is the first step in repairing your suit. There are two methods that you can use to reliably locate punctures. You can either inflate the suit, or use what we call the "*flashlight method*".

To locate a puncture by inflating the suit, you will need three heavy duty rubber bands and a spray bottle full of soapy water. To start, seal off the wrists and neck seal with heavy duty rubber bands. Close the zipper on the suit and the exhaust valve. If your suit has an automatic exhaust, screw the valve in all the way. Attach the suit inflator hose to your suit and blow up the suit until it is stiff (approximately 1 P.S.I. of pressure inside the suit).

Spray the suit with a solution of soapy water. Anywhere where there is a puncture, the surface of the suit should "bubble". You may also even be able to hear air escaping out of the leak, too. Mark the spot with a ball point pen by drawing a small circle around the puncture so you will be able to find it when you are ready to apply a patch. Be sure to rinse the soap off before you do any repair work.

The flashlight method of locating leaks also works well. The only item you will need to perform this test is a flashlight and a dark room. Take your suit into the darkened room and sit on the floor where you can spread the suit out comfortably. Hold a strong flashlight inside the suit and turn it on. Hold the lens of the flashlight against the inside surface of the suit and move it around in the area where you suspect the puncture to be located. The light will shine through the hole making the puncture very apparent in most cases.

In an emergency, you can patch most punctures with duct tape. Depending upon the type of suit or seals that you have, this may not always work well. Use duct tape only when you have no other patching material available and you must dive. Be sure to remove the duct tape immediately after you have completed your dive so that it doesn't leave a sticky residue on your suit.

Patching Vulcanized Rubber Suits

Vulcanized rubber dry suits can be patched very quickly, provided you have the proper patch materials with you. Most manufacturers have patch kits available for their suits that contains the glue and patches you will need to repair your suit. Be sure to follow the directions in the manual provided with your suit and/or repair kit.

Keep in mind that most glues have a shelf life and few are usable after 2 years, even if the container has not been opened. Also, many glues get thicker once the container has been opened and become difficult or impossible to use. Be sure to replace the glue in your repair kit periodically or it may not work when you need it.

For example, Viking's patches and glue are specifically designed to work together. The glue provided with the patch kit actually consists of two parts. One component is in the tube of glue while the other is on the back of the patch itself. If you try to use the glue supplied with a Viking repair kit with an ordinary piece of latex, or suit material, it will not stick because the catalyst is not present.

The most important points in patching a vulcanized rubber suit is to dry the suit surface. Use a towel to dry the outside of the suit quickly. Viking also recommends that you rough up the area where the patch is to be applied. Don't worry about the inside of the suit as long as you are only repairing a puncture.

Viking repair kits for vulcanized rubber suits include a piece of coarse sandpaper specifically for preparing the surface of the suit for patching. Rub the area vigorously where the patch is to be applied. Viking recommends that you actually remove the shiny surface layer of rubber and get down to the base material underneath. Unless you prepare the surface in this way,

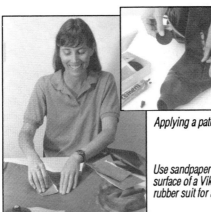

Applying a patch to a TLS suit.

Use sandpaper to prepare the surface of a Viking vulcanized rubber suit for a patch.

the patch will not stick. The area you prepare should be slightly larger than the patch itself since it is almost impossible to get the patch down with 100% precision.

Once you have applied the patch, rub it down vigorously. Although you can use your thumb for this, a wallpaper roller works much better. Be sure to rub around the outside edges of the patch.

Follow the directions on the glue provided with your patch kit regarding how long you should wait until you can dive again. With most repair patches and glue you can dive again after 5 minutes, but it takes several days for most adhesives to completely cure. Be sure to neutralize any excess glue with talcum powder to avoid getting glue on other parts of your suit.

Patching TLS and Other Coated Nylon Suits

TLS suits and other laminated materials can be patched very quickly. The materials you will need to repair a TLS suit include a small nylon brush, a rag, surface preparation solvent, glue, and a clean tin can (like an empty coffee can).

Patches are normally applied to the inside of these suits rather than to the exterior nylon. The surface is prepared using the cleaning solvent recommended by the manufacturer. To clean the surface, rub it vigorously with the rag dipped in the solvent. Allow the solvent to dry. Then apply the glue recommended by your suit's manufacturer. You won't need more than 1/6 cup of this mixture to apply a small patch.

Coat the area where the patch is to be applied and the patch itself. Allow the first coat to dry for 5 minutes. Apply a second coat and allow it to dry for 10 minutes. Apply the patch and rub it down with your thumb. The patch should be allowed to dry for at least 5 more minutes before you go back into the water.

To patch a crushed neoprene suit, carefully burn the nylon in a circle around the puncture.

Seam leaks in TLS or other urethane backed dry suits should be coated with a mixture of 50% Cotol and 50% Aquaseal. Apply 3 coats, allowing time for each coat to dry (usually 15-20 minutes). Allow the coating to dry until there is no liquid left in the material before you go back into the water. The drying time will vary with the temperature and humidity.

Patching Foam Neoprene

Repairing foam neoprene suits can be a bit more difficult than other types of dry suits. First, the suit must be completely dry before any permanent repair can be made. Due to the thick, cellular nature of this material, water and air don't always move through punctures in foam neoprene in a straight line. In addition, high wear areas in these suits, such as knees or armpits, often become spongy, making it necessary to replace whole sections of material.

Manufacturers such as Diving Unlimited International (DUI) have developed special techniques for plugging leaks in foam neoprene suits. They use a large, heavy-duty syringe to fill the puncture holes with Aquaseal®.

Repairing Crushed Neoprene Suits

Crushed neoprene dry suits can be patched easily, but they must be completely dry prior to making any permanent repair. Patches are normally applied to the inside of the suit, for both cosmetic and functional reasons. The nylon on the inside is also thinner than the exterior nylon and this makes repairs easier.

To patch a crushed neoprene suit, you will need a soldering iron, a white china marking pencil, patching material, an empty tin can, cleaning solvent, and Aquaseal. Mark the spot where the puncture is located by drawing a small circle around it with a white china marker. The circle should be the size of your patch. Use the soldering iron and carefully burn the nylon along the outer edge of the circle. Take special care not to burn a hole through the suit!

Dampen the area where the patch is to be applied to the suit with the cleaning solvent recommended by DUI. This will allow you to peel away the nylon inside the circle. Use DUI dry suit glue and apply it to both the patch and the area where the puncture is located. Allow the first coat to dry for five minutes, then apply a second coat to both parts. After ten minutes press the patch down. Wait at least another five minutes before diving, longer if possible.

A seam leak in a crushed neoprene dry suit or foam neoprene dry suit can be sealed very easily. Remove the nylon as previously explained and coat the seam with a mixture of 50% Cotol® and 50% Aquaseal®. Apply 2 coats of this mixture and allow to dry completely. Drying time will vary with temperature and humidity.

Neck Seal Replacement

Replacing a neck seal is a more time consuming process than patching a dry suit. Not more complicated, but definitely more time consuming. If you have never replaced a neck seal on a dry suit before you should allow yourself a full two hours to do the job. An experienced dry suit technician can probably do it in 45 minutes.

The techniques for repairing a neck seal will vary somewhat depending upon the type of suit and the seal material you select. Take your time; it's not difficult, but it must be done right. There is nothing more frustrating than replacing a seal and having it leak because you rushed the job.

Removing a Latex Seal from a Vulcanized Rubber Dry Suit

To get the best bond between a latex neck seal and a vulcanized rubber dry suit, you should remove the old neck seal and apply the new one to the outer surface. Although some manufacturers suggest attaching a latex neck seal to the lining of the suit, it's difficult and more time consuming to do this.

To remove an old latex neck seal from a vulcanized rubber dry suit that has been repaired using Viking's glue you'll need a blow dryer. This glue is heat activated and removal of latex parts is easiest when done this way.

Not all glues are heat activated, so check with the manufacturer of your suit if you aren't sure about your particular suit. The majority of the glues used on other suits will allow you to peel latex parts away from the suit without too much effort.

Viking uses a cloth tape covering the joint between the neck seal and the suit, remove this first. To remove this tape, heat it at the edge and carefully peel it back from the neck seal. Move the blow dryer back and forth over the tape and heat the suit gradually rather than holding it in one place. The tape should peel away easily if you do this properly.

Use a blow drier to remove tape and latex parts from a Viking suit that has been previously repaired with Viking glue.

Once the tape has been removed from the suit, start heating the old neck seal itself at the point where it joins the suit. Once the material begins to get warm, pull the neck seal away from the suit by stretching it in the opposite direction away from the body of the suit. Do not try to peel the neck seal back from the suit by turning it back on itself or lifting it away from the body of the suit. This action may cause the neck seal to pull the base material of the suit away from the lining and result in delamination of the material. Be patient or you will damage the base material.

Removing a Latex Seal from a Nylon Exterior Suit

Torn latex seals in good condition need not be completely removed from suits with nylon exteriors. If the seal material is in good shape, not cracked or gummy, simply cut the seal back to the edge of the suit, leaving the bottom edge of the old seal attached to the suit. The new seal can be glued directly to the remnant of the old one.

Latex seals that have deteriorated must be removed in order to get a good attachment to the base suit material. Peel the old seal away with a wire nippers with a blunt set of jaws. Take care to only grab the latex and not the base suit material. The material may come away in pieces so take your time and be patient.

Applying a Latex Neck Seal

To prepare a new latex neck seal, you will need sand paper and solvent. Rough up the neck seal for at least two inches back from the bottom edge all the way around on one side. If you intend to use cloth tape to finish the job you will need to sand the seal on both sides. Clean the sanded edge and the suit where the neck seal will be applied with the suit solvent recommended by the manufacturer of your suit.

Before you begin to apply glue to the neck seal of your suit there are a few other items that you will find very handy. As mentioned previously, a wallpaper roller is an invaluable aid in making dry suit repairs. Other items that you will find helpful are two neck seal templates and a thin sheet of clear plastic.

A neck seal template is a large, doughnut shaped ring cut from heavy plastic, cardboard, or plywood. The outside diameter of the ring should be equal to the base of a fully opened neck seal. The inside opening need be no larger than the inner opening of the neck seal.

Using neck seal templates will make neck seal installation much easier. To use the templates you attach the base of the neck seal to one of the templates with double sided tape. Transfer tape, available at office supply stores and made by 3M® works well for this purpose. The bottom edge of the neck seal should be flush with the outer edge of the template all the way around. While you are applying glue to the neck seal you can hold the assembly by the inside of the template to avoid getting glue on your fingers. Using the template also makes it much easier to apply the seal to your suit.

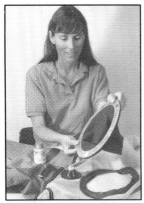

To make neck seal installation easier, attach the neck seal to a template. This will give the neck seal the proper shape and make it easier to handle.

The second template should be attached with two sided tape to the inside of the suit around the neck seal opening. This will give the opening the proper shape while you apply the neck seal to the outside. If you don't have a second template, spread the suit out flat and use dive weights to flatten the area on the suit where the neck seal will be applied and hold the suit in place. If the suit is not completely flat it will be difficult to apply the neck seal properly. Any pucker in the seal or the suit may create a channel for water that will cause the neck seal to leak.

If you are using a two part cement, such as the Viking glue, the cement is supplied in a can and the hardener is supplied in a bottle. The Viking hardener is extremely toxic. Wear rubber gloves while handling this material and avoid getting it on your skin, in your eyes, or inhaling the fumes.

Work with good ventilation. Use only a few drops of the Viking hardener to a cup of cement. More hardener is not better. Wipe the threads on the hardener bottle if you have gotten any hardener on them. Otherwise, the hardener will seal the lid to the bottle and you will not be able to remove it when you need to use it again.

Mix the cement and hardener thoroughly and brush it onto the outside of the suit and inside of the neck seal. Allow time between each coat to dry. Apply as many coats as is recommended by the manufacturer. When the last coat is tacky, lay a sheet of thin clear plastic over the suit at the neck seal opening. Position the template and neck seal where you want it before you remove the plastic. The plastic allows you to align the seal without having it stick to the suit.

Use a wallpaper roller to help rub the seal down on the suit.

Installing a neoprene neck seal.

Pull the plastic away a little at a time and press the template and neck seal onto the suit. Use a roller on the seal to further ensure a good bond. Remove the inner and outer template. Then use the roller again.

Coat the inside and the outside of the seal with pure talcum powder to neutralize any excess glue. Remember to trim latex neck seals before you use them the for the first time.

You can dive immediately if you must, but the seal will be more reliable the longer you wait. After 24 hours the glue will be fully cured.

When you don't have a template available you can still install a latex neck seal but it is much more difficult. Before you start your glue job, place the neck seal on the suit and see where it should lie. Mark the suit and the seal at 4 points, 90 degrees apart. Glue the seal to the suit at each of the four points. Then gently stretch the seal down onto the suit so that it lays flat. It helps to have another person to hold things in position.

Seam Tape

Seam tape is sometimes applied to Viking suits and other vulcanized rubber dry suits. The tape is a cement impregnated cloth tape. The main purpose of the tape is for cosmetic appearances although it does afford some additional chafing protection for the base of the seal.

To apply seam tape the outer surface of the seal must be sanded prior to installation on the suit. Cut the tape to the appropriate length for the seal. Apply two coats of glue to the tape and the neck seal. When the second coat of glue is dry place the tape on the suit and use the roller to make it stick well. Apply pure talcum powder to neutralize any excess glue.

Replacing a Foam Neoprene Seal on Foam Neoprene Dry Suits

Foam neoprene seals are removed from neoprene dry suits by cutting the seal away from the suit. Use the largest, sharpest scissors available. Cut just behind the existing seam, removing a thin sliver of the base material of the suit itself. Your objective is to have a clean attachment point for the new seal.

Before you begin any repairs the suit must be completely dry, both inside and outside. To attach the new seal you will need a white china marker, neoprene cement, Cotol® and Aquaseal®. Mark the edge of the new seal and the suit opening with a white china marker every 90 degrees so that there are 4 marks for alignment.

Apply 3 coats of glue to the edge of the neck seal where it will join the suit and the neck seal opening on the suit itself. When the last coat of glue is tacky, join the neck seal to the suit by aligning the white index marks you made on the two parts. The edge of the seal butts to the edge of the suit.

Join the seal to the suit by just sticking them together gently. This will allow you to see if all of the marks are properly aligned. If everything does not line up you can still pull them apart easily at this point. Once things are properly aligned, pinch the two edges together to ensure a good bond.

Allow the suit to sit for another hour. Then apply a coating of 50% Cotol® and 50% Aquaseal® to the inside of the seam where the seal joins the suit. This method of replacing a foam neoprene seal on a neoprene suit applies to both neck seals and wrist seals.

Remember to stretch foam neoprene neck seals before you use them for the first time. Never trim a neoprene neck or wrist seal.

Replacing Neoprene Seals on Other Dry Suits

Neoprene seals will stick to other dry suit materials but may require more glue to be properly attached. For example, using Viking glue and a neoprene neck seals on a vulcanized rubber suit may require up to 20 coats of glue for proper application. Consult the manufacturer of your suit for proper techniques for your particular suit and seals.

Replacing Latex Wrist Seals

To replace a latex wrist seal you will need the new seal, sand paper, masking tape, solvent, cement, a 2 liter plastic soda bottle, and a sheet of thin, clear plastic (such as a plastic bag). Be sure to have all the materials on hand before you start the job.

Prep the seal by sanding it along its bottom edge on one side. Or, sand both sides if you will be using seam tape. A strip one inch wide should be buffed until it is visibly rougher than the shiny black appearance of new latex. Without adequate sanding the seal will not adhere to the suit properly. Clean the seal with whatever solvent is recommended by the manufacturer.

Insert the plastic soda bottle (or any device of a similar diameter) inside the sleeve. The bottom end of the soda bottle should protrude for at least three inches past the end of the sleeve. Hold the bottle in position by

Stretch the wrist seal over whatever device you use as a plug for attaching it.

Apply the glue to the seal and the sleeve.

applying masking tape around the outside of the sleeve 3 or 4 inches back from the end of the sleeve.

Stretch the new seal over the bottle and onto the sleeve where you want it to be when the job is complete. There should be approximately 1 inch of seal material covering the sleeve all the way around. Next, fold the bottom edge of the seal back onto itself so that there is 1 inch of material folded over. The fold itself should be butted up to the end of the sleeve. Apply masking tape over the wrist seal below the fold to hold the seal in position.

Apply glue evenly on both the seal and the sleeve. Be sure to use a thin coat of glue on both parts and apply as many coats as the manufacturer recommends, depending upon the type of glue you are using. When the last coat is tacky, wrap the sleeve with the clear plastic down to the bottom edge.

Unfold the wrist seal back down on top of the sleeve. When you are sure you have the correct alignment, pull the plastic away, tacking the seal down as you go. Use a wall paper roller and roll the sleeve to ensure a good bond between the seal and the sleeve. Apply pure talcum powder to neutralize any excess glue.

Zipper Replacement

Zipper replacement is normally a factory repair job, due to the extreme importance of the integrity of the dry suit zipper. You should only attempt a zipper replacement if you are in a remote location where you will be unable to dive unless you repair the suit yourself.

If you will be traveling to a remote location where you anticipate the possibility of a zipper replacement contact the manufacturer of your dry suit. In all likelihood they will be happy to train you in zipper replacement techniques.

Valve Overhaul

Dry suit valves should be serviced on an annual basis at the same time you have your regulator serviced. Your dry suit dealer will have the right tools and spares to ensure that the job is done properly. *Dry suit repair technicians should consult the manufacturers of the suits they must repair to obtain the latest specifications for valve repair. Since valve materials and specifications change frequently, the information presented here is only a general overview of valve design and how they work.*

In this section we will show the service procedures for some of the more common, typical valves. *We present this information here as reference material for qualified dry suit technicians and for advanced divers who want to understand how dry suit valves work. Under no circumstances should an untrained person attempt to service dry suit valves.*

We will use the language used by the valve manufacturers in their drawings to describe the parts. In certain cases, this may differ from common terminology used in the U.S. For example, S.I. Tech may refer to a valve body as a "valve housing", or an inflator nipple as a "male connector". We will attempt to clarify or use alternate terms wherever possible.

GSD Inflator Valve

The GSD valves were used on DUI suits during the 1980's. Servicing the GSD inflator valve requires a pair of ordinary pliers, a rag, and a pair of circlip pliers.

The valve may be removed from the suit by unscrewing the mount nut on the inside of the suit. Take care to set aside any shim plates that are present. On certain types of suits, such as TLS suits, the valve may be mounted on the suit with silicone sealant. Remove any traces of the old sealant by peeling it off before mounting the valve back on the suit.

The inflator valve stem may be removed with a wrench to replace the o-ring. Discard the old o-ring, clean the valve with a dilute solution of soap and water, and replace the o-ring.

To service the body of the valve, start by removing the outer ring. The part unscrews and you will probably need a pair of channel locks and a rag to do this properly. At this point you will be able to remove the button, membrane pin, and inlet diaphragm as a single unit. Clean these parts with a dilute solution of soap and water. Rinse thoroughly with fresh water. Replace any parts that are worn. Look for wear on the o-rings or diaphragm.

Remove the membrane body by unscrewing it with the circlip pliers. This will give you access to the membrane, flapper housing and flapper.

The button, membrane pin, and inlet diaphragm are removed as a single unit.

Removal of the exterior exhaust nut from a GSD push-to-dump valve.

Removing the membrane body from the GSD inflator valve.

Clean these parts with soap and water. Rinse thoroughly with fresh water. Replace any parts that are worn.

To reassemble the valve, install the flapper, followed by the flapper housing, the membrane, the membrane body, and the slip-on nut. Be sure the membrane is installed properly. The base of the membrane is wider than the top.

Install the inlet diaphragm (wide end down), the membrane pin and button as a single unit. Screw down the outer ring until snug by hand and tighten another 1/2 turn using pliers and a rag. Reinstall the valve stem and tighten until snug. Mount the valve back on the suit using silicone sealant if required. Check the operation of the valve carefully before using the suit underwater again. The valve should operate smoothly.

GSD Push-to-dump Exhaust

To service both the GSD exhaust valves you will need a rag and two large pairs of pliers. These valves are not complicated, but they do have quite a few parts. These valves may be removed from a suit by unscrewing the mount nut on the inside of the suit.

Remove the exterior exhaust nut by holding the nut with a rag and a pair of pliers. Unscrew the nut while you hold the valve base.

When the nut is removed you can then lift it together with the valve body off the valve base. This will expose the interior components of the valve.

Lift off the inner gear and compression spring. This will expose the interior assembly that includes the button, exhaust diaphragm, and other parts. Hold the button in one hand and place a rag on the nut at the bottom of the assembly. Grip the nut with a pliers and unscrew it.

Separate the button, spring, spring base, o-ring, exhaust diaphragm, exhaust plate, o-ring, and nut. Discard the o-rings and diaphragm. Clean all parts with soap and water, and rinse thoroughly. Replace the o-rings and diaphragm. Do not lubricate the silicone diaphragm. Reassemble the parts and tighten until snug with the pliers.

Lift the valve body off the base.

Wash the valve base, body, and compression spring with soap and water. Replace the gasket in the valve base. Place the button/exhaust diaphragm assembly in the valve base so it rests against the seal. Drop the spring over the button/diaphragm assembly, followed by the inner gear. The inner gear must

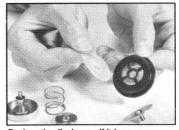
Replace the diaphragm if it is worn.

be aligned to that its teeth engage the slots in the valve base.

Place the exterior exhaust nut and body of the valve in position over the compression spring. Push down on the body and screw the exterior exhaust nut down until it is snug. Install the valve back on the suit (with silicone sealant if needed). Test the valve for proper operation before

Check the gasket in the valve base and replace if necessary.

using it underwater again.

GSD Automatic Exhaust

The GSD automatic exhaust valve is very similar to the GSD push-to-dump valve. Many of the parts are interchangeable making stocking inventory for these parts inexpensive. The service procedures are also much alike.

Remove the exterior exhaust nut by holding the nut with a rag and a pair of pliers. Unscrew the nut while you hold the valve base. When the nut is removed you can then lift it together with the valve body off the valve base. This will expose the interior components of the valve.

Install the button/exhaust diaphragm assembly in the valve base.

Lift off the adjustment spring. The locking inner gear may remain in the adjustable body. It is not necessary to remove it unless it is damaged, or there is sand or corrosion underneath making it difficult to turn. It may be possible to run water underneath it and clean it out without removing it. If

Inspect the exhaust diaphragm and replace it if worn.

you must remove it, use a pliers to gently pull it out. Work each leg of the gear a bit at a time. Do not attempt to pull it out by pulling on one gear only.

The interior diaphragm assembly that includes the button, the two exhaust diaphragms, and other parts will be exposed when you remove the adjustable body. Hold the button in one hand and place a rag on the nut at the bottom of the assembly. Grip the nut with a pliers and unscrew it. Remove both exhaust diaphragms and replace them. Remove both o-rings; in the spring base and the valve base. Discard the o-rings.

Clean all parts with soap and water. Rinse thoroughly with fresh water. Install new o-rings and exhaust diaphragms. Assemble the button, spring, spring base, exhaust plate, and nut. Tighten with a pliers, using a rag to prevent damage to the parts.

Place the interior diaphragm assembly back in the valve base. Be sure the o-ring is installed in the base. Slide the adjustment spring over the diaphragm assembly, followed by the adjustable body and exterior exhaust nut. Tighten the exterior exhaust nut by holding it with a rag as you use a pliers to apply gentle force.

Install the valve on the suit using interior gaskets and/or silicone sealant as required. Test the valve for proper operation prior to using the suit for diving.

S.I. Tech Inflator Valve

The S.I. Tech inflator valve has been used on DUI suits since 1990. It is a very simple valve to maintain. All of the wrenches and measurements on S.I. Tech valves are metric.

Remove the valve from the suit by unscrewing the valve mounting plate. Separate the valve from the suit. On some suits it may be mounted with silicone cement. The old cement will need to be removed and new cement applied when it is time to reinstall the valve.

Remove the inflator nipple with a wrench. Discard the old o-ring at the base of the inflator nipple.

Unscrew the valve stem from the valve button. Hold the valve button using a pliers with a thin rag underneath it so as not to damage the button. Place a socket on the bottom of the brass valve stem and unscrew. This will expose the valve seat on the stem and the spring.

Remove the o-ring on the valve button and discard. Clean the valve parts with a dilute solution of soap and water. Examine the valve seat and stem. If they are worn they should be replaced.

Lubricate the new o-rings and valve stem with silicone grease. Install them in the inflator nipple and on the valve button. Thread the valve nipple into the valve body and tighten until snug. Do not overtighten.

Install the spring in the valve body, followed by the inflator button. Put the valve stem into the valve body and thread it into the inflator button. Hold

Disassembly of the S.I. Tech inflator valve used on DUI suits.

the button with a rag and a pair of pliers. Tighten the valve stem with a socket. Install the valve on the suit, with silicone sealant if required. Test the valve for correct operation prior to diving.

Viking PRO Inflator Valve

The Viking PRO Inflator valve is also manufactured by S.I. Tech. The valve is very rugged and easy to maintain.

Remove the valve from the suit by unscrewing the nut on the inside of the suit. Take care not to lose the while plastic washer that seals inside the suit or the spring.

Use a wrench to remove the male connector (inflator nipple) from the valve housing (body). Remove the o-ring and discard it.

Hold the push button (inflator button) with a pliers and a rag. On some suits there may be a plastic sleeve surrounding the valve button that must be pried out of the valve body first before you can grasp the button. Turn the valve stem with a socket wrench until it is separated from the inflator button. Remove the o-ring and center guide from the exterior part of the valve body. Remove the valve stem and washer.

Removal of the valve stem from a Viking PRO inflator valve.

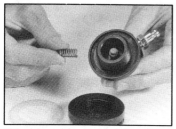

This spring must engage both the valve stem and the mount nut for this valve to work properly.

Discard the o-ring and examine the center guide and washer. Replace the guide and washer if needed.

Clean all metal and plastic parts with a dilute solution of soap and water. Rinse thoroughly. Lubricate all internal parts and o-rings with a light coating of silicone grease.

Thread the inflator nipple into the valve body. Make sure the o-ring is in position. Install the washer on the valve stem and insert the stem through the valve body. Place the center guide on the stem. The o-ring should be installed on the button. Thread the button on the stem and tighten with the socket.

Install the valve on the suit through the appropriate opening. Put the spring on the plastic nipple inside the mount nut. The spring must engage both the mount nut and the valve stem for the valve to operate properly. Without the spring in position the suit will inflate continuously when the inflator hose is connected. If the hose is not connected and the spring is not in position the suit will leak through the valve and the diver will get wet.

Make sure the white plastic washer is installed on the threads of the valve body. Tighten the nut by hand until it is snug. Test the valve by connecting the inflator and depressing the button several times prior to diving. The valve should operate smoothly and not stick.

Viking Sport Inflator Valve

The Viking Sport valve is also manufactured by S.I. Tech. The two components of the valve, i.e., the valve head and the valve connector, should be serviced at the same time.

To remove the valve connector (body) from the suit, turn the locking washer inside the suit as you hold the connector housing on the outside of the suit. The valve may be sticky and adhere to the suit but can easily be pried away. Set the distance washer that was under the locking washer inside the suit aside for safe keeping.

Insert a hex key in the locking "screw" and remove it from the valve body. The hole that runs through this "screw" is actually the air passage into the suit. By removing the "screw" you will expose the "ball" in the other end of it. This ball together with the piston in the hose actually control the flow of air into the suit.

Remove the o-ring that holds the ball and the spring behind it. Discard the o-ring. Clean the ball, the spring, and the orifice with a dilute solution of soap and water. You may want to run a pipe cleaner through the screw to clean out any encrusting deposits due to salt or sand.

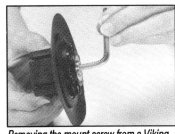
Removing the mount screw from a Viking Sport valve.

Lubricate the spring and ball with a light coat of silicone grease. Install them in the screw, followed by a new o-ring to hold them in place. Insert the connector housing through the hole in the suit. Place the distance washer over the opening in the connector housing.

This ball controls the air flow in a Viking Sport valve.

Thread the screw and locking washer assembly back into the valve body. Tighten until snug with the hex key.

The only service the end user will normally perform on the valve head will be to replace the two external o-rings. It is easy to identify when these are worn.

To service the inside of the head at the end of the hose, use a soft jaw vice to hold the wrench flats on the base of the head. Cushion the head itself with a rag and remove with a pair of vice grips. Clean the piston and springs with soap and water. Replace all 3 o-rings. Reassemble and tighten the head until snug,

Be sure to thoroughly test the valve before diving.

S.I. Tech Exhaust Valve

The S.I. Tech Exhaust Valve is used on Viking suits, DUI suits, and many others. There are no tools required to service this valve except for a strong, thin bladed knife. The knife should not be sharp.

Before you can service this valve you must remove it from the suit. Hold the body of the valve outside the suit while you reach inside the suit and unscrew the locking screw. If you are working on a Viking suit, do not lose the white plastic gasket that seals the valve inside the suit. Be sure to hold the valve by its protective cover or the whole valve may come apart at this point.

If the valve does not easily come apart, screw the locking screw back into the valve a few turns. Turn the lid of the valve until it is at the maximum open position. Place your thumbs on the base of the locking screw and pull down on the protective cover. The protective cover should separate itself from the rest of the valve and you can continue disassembly. Unscrew the locking screw again if needed.

Remove the large push spring and the protective cover and set them aside.

The next step must be done very carefully in order to prevent damage to the valve and to keep from hurting yourself.

Insert a dull, thin bladed knife, or a screwdriver, between the lid of the valve and the locking ring. Pry up on the locking ring very gently and care-

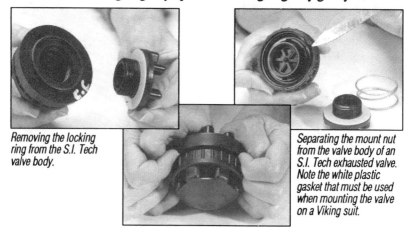

Removing the locking ring from the S.I. Tech valve body.

Separating the mount nut from the valve body of an S.I. Tech exhausted valve. Note the white plastic gasket that must be used when mounting the valve on a Viking suit.

To remove the protective cover from the valve, you may need to use the mount nut for leverage as shown here, particularly on older valves.

fully. Do not attempt to pry the locking ring out of its groove at one point all at once. Instead, work the knife around the ring slowly, prying the ring upwards a little bit at a time. If you pry too much of the ring at any one time you will crack or break the locking ring. The locking ring must be replaced if this happens. Remove the locking ring once it is free of its groove.

Hold the lid of the valve and unscrew the locking nut and groove ring from the lid by pulling gently on the locking nut as you turn it. Several other parts will come away at the same time.

Lift the groove ring off of the locking nut. This will expose the membrane (gasket). Check the membrane for signs of wear and replace if necessary. Examine the back valve (flapper valve) that seats against the opening in the locking nut. If it is worn or cracked it should be replaced. Do not lubricate these parts with silicone grease.

With the groove ring removed, the membrane and back valve are accessible.

Reassembly of the S.I. Tech exhaust valve.

Removal of the piston and control spring from the lid.

Remove the piston from the lid. Examine the center guide and control spring. Clean all of the plastic parts and metal springs with a dilute solution of soap and water. Rinse thoroughly. Place the control spring back in the lid making sure the center guide engages it. Lower the piston into position.

Position the locking nut in the groove ring. Make sure both the back valve and the membrane are in place. Holding the locking nut, screw it into the lid deep enough so the locking ring may be wedged into position. Carefully install the locking ring into its groove by compressing it gently. If it breaks it must be replaced.

Drop the push spring into the protective cover and compress the valve mechanisms between the lid and the protective cover. Position the valve on the suit and thread the locking screw into the valve body.

If you are working on a Viking suit make sure the white plastic gasket is between the locking screw and the suit or water will leak into the suit. If you are working on another type of suit you may need to apply silicone sealant underneath the protective cover to seal the valve to the suit. Check with the manufacturer of the suit for specific instructions in regard to mounting this valve. Always test the valve for correct operation before using the suit for diving again.

White's /Apeks Inflator

White's and Apeks inflator valves are very similar to each other. Service to these valves usually involves both cleaning and o-ring replacement.

Remove the backing plate that is used to mount the valve on the suit by unscrewing it. Separate the valve body from the suit.

Use a screwdriver or a pair of pliers and carefully pry the circlip off the valve stem. This will allow you to remove the valve stem from the valve body. This will also give you access to the spring.

Use a wrench to remove the inflator nipple from the valve body. Take care no to damage the mating surface where the inflator hose couples to the nipple.

Remove the o-rings from the valve stem and inflator nipple. Clean all of the plastic and metal parts with a dilute solution of soap and water. Lightly lubricate new o-rings for the valve stem and inflator nipple and install them.

With the circlip off you can remove the valve stem from the White's valve.

Thread the nipple back into the valve body and tighten until snug. Install the spring in the valve body and insert the valve stem through it. Push the stem through the valve body until you can reinstall the circlip. Mount the valve back on the suit as per the suit manufacturer's instructions and test the valve before using it in open water.

White's /Apeks Exhaust

As mentioned previously, the White's and Apeks exhaust valves are almost identical in appearance and function. Both are very similar internally to the S.I. Tech exhaust valve. A brief look at the mechanism of the Apeks valve is presented here.

Remove the valve from the suit by unscrewing the backing plate for the valve from the valve body. Remove the three screws in the base of the valve body with a Phillips head screwdriver. Remove the large exhaust spring from the valve body.

Unscrew the spring retainer and diaphragm retainer together and remove them from the screw cap. Examine and replace the non-return diaphragm as needed. Check and replace the silicone gasket if necessary. Remove the exhaust seat, small spring retainer, and small exhaust spring. Clean all metal and plastic parts with a dilute solution of soap and water. Rinse all parts thoroughly with clean fresh water.

Place the small exhaust spring, the small spring retainer, and the exhaust seat back in the screw cap. Assemble the large spring retainer and the diaphragm retainer together. Make sure the silicone gasket and non-return diaphragm are in place. Screw the spring retainer back into the cap. Place the large spring inside the valve body.

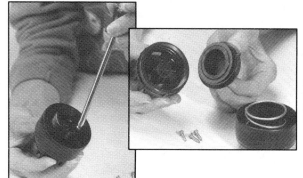

Remove the spring retainer and diaphragm retainer together.

Use a Phillips head screwdriver to remove the three screws in the base of Apeks valve.

When properly assembled, the arrow inside the exhaust valve body must align with the start of the thread on the outside rim of the large spring retainer when fitting the spline. When these parts are properly mated, thread the three screws into the exhaust valve body and tighten until snug. Install the valve on the suit according to the suit manufacturer's directions. Test the valve carefully prior to diving.

Examine all gaskets and the diaphragm and replace if necessary.

Reinstalling the small exhaust spring.

Appendix A

Thermal Guidelines

The Sport Thermal Guidelines were created to allow divers to predict the performance of a wetsuit or dry suit, given the diver's individual characteristics, anticipated work rate, the depth, and temperature of the water. *These tables are meant as a point of reference only. You will need to experiment to determine your own insulation needs.*

We define work rates as follows:

Work Rate	Example
Light	Taking photographs or observing surroundings.
Moderate	Normal swimming.
Heavy	Strong swimming or dragging an object across the bottom. Most divers can only do this for short periods.

The first step in determining the correct amount of insulation for various thermal conditions is to determine your "Plus Rating". Your Plus Rating is a conversion factor for your body size that helps us to compute your insulation needs. You will use your Plus Rating to choose your personal insulation guide.

Plus Rating Table

YOUR BODY WEIGHT IN POUNDS			90	105	120	135	150	165	180	195	210	225	245
YOUR PLUS RATING IN DEGREES	-4	-2	0	+2	+4	+6	+8	+10	+12	+14	+16	+18	+20

Directions for the Plus Rating Table:

1) Find your body weight in the table and read the corresponding Plus Rating below it.

2) Ask yourself, " When I am in a room where the temperature is comfortable for the 'average' person, am I comfortable? Or, do I feel colder, or warmer, than others?"

a) If you are comfortable, use your plus rating with no corrections in the following Personal Insulation Prediction tables.

b) If you are too warm, ask yourself, "Would I need an open collar shirt and loose clothing to be comfortable?" If your answer is "Yes!", select a plus rating that is 2 degrees higher. For example, move from Plus 10 to Plus 12 for a 165 pound man. If you normally perspire in a room where others are comfortable then move yourself up 4 degrees in the Plus Rating Table.

c) If you feel colder than the average person, ask yourself, "Would I need to wear a long sleeve shirt? If so, then move yourself down 2 degrees in the Plus Rating table. For example, a 165 pound man under these circumstances would consider himself a Plus 8 in stead of a Plus 10. If you need a sweater to be comfortable, then move yourself down 4 degrees in the Plus Rating.

d) If you are using a crushed neoprene or foam neoprene dry suit, move your Plus Rating 4 degrees higher due to the intrinsic insulation in these suits.

CAUTION:

There are very few people whose metabolism is so low or so high to cause them to require a plus or minus 4 degrees beyond what their normal body size dictates in the tables.

Directions for Using the Personal Insulation Prediction Tables

1) After you have obtained your plus rating from the Plus Rating Table, locate the Personal Insulation Prediction Table that corre sponds to your Plus Rating.

2) Locate the expected water temperature of your dive site.

3) Determine what level of diving activity you intend to pursue dur ing your dive.

4) Read to the right to determine what level of insulation you will need to dive.

5) *Example:* A diver with a Plus Rating of 4 intends to do underwater photography in 76 degree water. That diver will need to wear a dry suit and 50-65 degree Thinsulate® to stay comfortable during that dive.

CAUTION: *These guidelines may not be totally accurate for every diver. They must be tested to insure they meet the user's needs.*

CAUTION: *Your weight requirements will vary as you change your insulation.*

CAUTION: *It is better to under-insulate than over-insulate.*

Personal Insulation Prediction Table
Dry Suit 0 Diver , Nominal Weight = 90 pounds

	Diving Activity			Insulation Level Required
	Heavy	**Moderate**	**Light**	
Water Temperature	84	88	92	Expeditionary weight polypropylene underwear
Water Temperature	74	82	86	Single layer of bunting or lightweight pile
Water Temperature	64	73	80	50-65 degree Thinsulate ®
Water Temperature	57	68	76	Double weight bunting heavy weight pile, or Open Cell Foam
Water Temperature	44	58	70	35-50 degree Thinsulate ®

Water temperature in degrees Fahrenheit.

Personal Insulation Prediction Table

Dry Suit +2 Diver, Nominal Weight = 105 pounds

	Diving Activity			Insulation Level Required
	Heavy	**Moderate**	**Light**	
Water Temperature	82	86	90	Expeditionary weight polypropylene underwear
Water Temperature	72	80	84	Single layer of bunting or lightweight pile
Water Temperature	62	71	78	50–65 degree Thinsulate ®
Water Temperature	55	66	74	Double weight bunting, heavy weight pile, or Open Cell Foam
Water Temperature	42	56	68	35–50 degree Thinsulate ®

Water temperature in degrees Fahrenheit.

Personal Insulation Prediction Table

Dry Suit +4 Diver , Nominal Weight = 120 pounds

	Diving Activity			Insulation Level Required
	Heavy	**Moderate**	**Light**	
Water Temperature	80	84	88	Expeditionary weight polypropylene underwear
Water Temperature	70	78	82	Single layer of bunting or lightweight pile
Water Temperature	60	69	76	50–65 degree Thinsulate ®
Water Temperature	53	64	72	Double weight bunting heavy weight pile, or Open Cell Foam
Water Temperature	40	54	66	35–50 degree Thinsulate ®

Water temperature in degrees Fahrenheit.

Personal Insulation Prediction Table

Dry Suit +6 Diver, Nominal Weight = 135 pounds

| | Diving Activity | | | Insulation Level Required |
	Heavy	Moderate	Light	
Water Temperature	78	82	86	Expeditionary weight polypropylene underwear
Water Temperature	68	76	80	Single layer of bunting or lightweight pile
Water Temperature	58	67	74	50-65 degree Thinsulate ®
Water Temperature	51	62	70	Double weight bunting, heavy weight pile, or Open Cell Foam
Water Temperature	38	52	64	35-50 degree Thinsulate ®

Water temperature in degrees Fahrenheit.

Personal Insulation Prediction Table

Dry Suit +8 Diver , Nominal Weight = 150 pounds

| | Diving Activity | | | Insulation Level Required |
	Heavy	Moderate	Light	
Water Temperature	76	80	84	Expeditionary weight polypropylene underwear
Water Temperature	66	74	78	Single layer of bunting or lightweight pile
Water Temperature	56	65	72	50-65 degree Thinsulate ®
Water Temperature	493	60	68	Double weight bunting heavy weight pile, or Open Cell Foam
Water Temperature	36	50	62	35-50 degree Thinsulate ®

Water temperature in degrees Fahrenheit.

Personal Insulation Prediction Table

Dry Suit +10 Diver, Nominal Weight = 165 pounds

	Diving Activity			Insulation Level Required
	Heavy	**Moderate**	**Light**	
Water Temperature	74	78	82	Expeditionary weight polypropylene underwear
Water Temperature	64	72	76	Single layer of bunting or lightweight pile
Water Temperature	54	63	70	50–65 degree Thinsulate ®
Water Temperature	47	58	66	Double weight bunting, heavy weight pile, or Open Cell Foam
Water Temperature	34	48	0	35–50 degree Thinsulate ®

Water temperature in degrees Fahrenheit.

Personal Insulation Prediction Table

Dry Suit +12 Diver , Nominal Weight = 180 pounds

	Diving Activity			Insulation Level Required
	Heavy	**Moderate**	**Light**	
Water Temperature	72	76	80	Expeditionary weight polypropylene underwear
Water Temperature	62	70	74	Single layer of bunting or lightweight pile
Water Temperature	52	61	68	50–65 degree Thinsulate ®
Water Temperature	45	56	64	Double weight bunting heavy weight pile, or Open Cell Foam
Water Temperature	32	46	58	35–50 degree Thinsulate ®

Water temperature in degrees Fahrenheit.

Personal Insulation Prediction Table

Dry Suit +14 Diver, Nominal Weight = 195 pounds

	Diving Activity			Insulation Level Required
	Heavy	**Moderate**	**Light**	
Water Temperature	70	74	78	Expeditionary weight polypropylene underwear
Water Temperature	60	68	72	Single layer of bunting or lightweight pile
Water Temperature	50	59	66	50–65 degree Thinsulate ®
Water Temperature	43	54	62	Double weight bunting, heavy weight pile, or Open Cell Foam
Water Temperature	30	44	56	35–50 degree Thinsulate ®

Water temperature in degrees Fahrenheit.

Personal Insulation Prediction Table

Dry Suit +16 Diver , Nominal Weight = 200 pounds

	Diving Activity			Insulation Level Required
	Heavy	**Moderate**	**Light**	
Water Temperature	68	72	76	Expeditionary weight polypropylene underwear
Water Temperature	58	66	70	Single layer of bunting or lightweight pile
Water Temperature	48	57	64	50–65 degree Thinsulate ®
Water Temperature	41	52	60	Double weight bunting heavy weight pile, or Open Cell Foam
Water Temperature	28	42	54	35–50 degree Thinsulate ®

Water temperature in degrees Fahrenheit.

Personal Insulation Prediction Table

Dry Suit +18 Diver, Nominal Weight = 225 pounds

	Diving Activity			Insulation Level Required
	Heavy	**Moderate**	**Light**	
Water Temperature	66	70	74	Expeditionary weight polypropylene underwear
Water Temperature	56	64	68	Single layer of bunting or lightweight pile
Water Temperature	46	55	62	50-65 degree Thinsulate ®
Water Temperature	39	50	58	Double weight bunting, heavy weight pile, or Open Cell Foam
Water Temperature	26	40	52	35-50 degree Thinsulate ®

Water temperature in degrees Fahrenheit.

Personal Insulation Prediction Table

Dry Suit +20 Diver, Nominal Weight = 245 pounds

	Diving Activity			Insulation Level Required
	Heavy	**Moderate**	**Light**	
Water Temperature	64	68	72	Expeditionary weight polypropylene underwear
Water Temperature	54	62	66	Single layer of bunting or lightweight pile
Water Temperature	44	53	60	50-65 degree Thinsulate ®
Water Temperature	37	48	56	Double weight bunting heavy weight pile, or Open Cell Foam
Water Temperature	24	38	50	35-50 degree Thinsulate ®

Water temperature in degrees Fahrenheit.

Appendix B

Dry Suit and Accessory Manufacturers

SUPPLIER	PRODUCTS AND SERVICES
Amron International Diving Supply, Inc. 759 West Fourth Ave. Escondido, CA 92025 Telephone: 619-746-3834 FAX: 619-746-1508	U.S. distributor Nokia dry suit Manufactures undergarments
Diving Unlimited International, Inc. 1148 Delevan Dr. San Diego, CA 92102 Telephone: 800-325-8439 FAX: 619-237-0378	All types of dry suits: exclusive mfg. of crushed neoprene dry suits. Thinsulate & pile understand Complete repair facility.
Harvey's Skin Diving Suits, Inc. 2505 South 252nd Street Telephone: 206-824-1114 FAX: 206-824-3323	Foam neoprene dry suits Urethane coated nylon dry suits Pile undergarments.
Mobby's USA 4625 Nevso Ave. Suite 1 Las Vegas, NV 89103 Telephone: 702-364-4998 FAX: 702-364-9974	Neoprene dry suits Urethane coated nylon dry suits

SUPPLIER	PRODUCTS AND SERVICES
Ocean Bottoms - Mountain Tops 182 Purdy Dr. Punta Gorda, FL 33980 Telephone: 813-624-4359 FAX: 813-743-0730	Radiant insulating undergarments Viking repair facility
Parkway/Imperial 241 Raritan Street South Amboy, NJ 08879 Telephone: 908-721-5300 FAX: 908-721-4016	Foam neoprene dry suits Vulcanized rubber dry suits
SAS Wetsuits 530 Sixth Street Hermosa Beach, CA 90254 Telephone: 213-374-4074 FAX: 213-372-7457	Foam neoprene dry suits
Scubapro 3105 E. Harcourt Rancho Dominguez, CA 90221 Telephone: 213- 639-7850 FAX: 213-605-0293	U.S. distributer for White's dry suits Pile undergarments
Seatec 2035 California Ave. Corona, CA 91718 Telephone: 714-734-6850 FAX: 714-734-3214	Urethane coated nylon dry suits Pile undergarments
Trelleborg - Viking 30700 Solon Industrial Parkway Solon, OH 44139 Telephone: 216-349-1319 FAX: 216-248-6936	Vulcanized rubber dry suits Open cell foam underwear
Whitehouse Industries 1106 Market Street Pocomoke City, MD 21581 Telephone: 301-957-4417	Urethane coated nylon & TLS dry suits Pile undergarments Complete repair facility
White's Scubapro Ltd. 6820 Kirkpatrick, RR#3 Victoria, B.C. Canada V8X3X1 Telephone: 604-652-5510 FAX: 604-652-5543	Urethane coated nylon dry suits Pile undergarments

Glossary of Dry Suit Diving Terms

a

active heating systems: Any diver heating system that relies on an external, heat source. Examples include electrically heated suits, hot water suits, and chemically heated suits.

argon: A heavy inert gas that provides better insulation capabilities than air. Argon is absorbed across the skin and may affect normal decompression. Diving with argon in a dry suit is considered experimental at this time.

automatic exhaust valve: A valve that will vent air from the diver's dry suit when the valve is adjusted properly and is at the shallowest depth in relation to the diver's body. This valve is usually mounted on the left upper arm.

b

"blind" stitch: A construction technique where a sewing stitch does not penetrate both sides of the suit.

c

Clo: A Clo unit is the amount of thermal insulation that is required to maintain an "average" resting man in thermal balance in an air environment where the temperature is 70 degrees F, the relative humidity is less than 50%, and the air movement is 20 feet per minute.

closed circuit rebreather: A breathing apparatus that recirculates the breathing gas and removes carbon dioxide from the system. These devices do not emit bubbles and are frequently used by military divers.

constant volume dry suit: A dry suit that maintains the same internal air volume regardless of the depth.

contamination reduction corridor: A confined area where personnel and equipment are decontaminated

contamination reduction zone: In a spill of toxic chemicals, the contamination reduction zone is the area where the diver is washed down prior to removing his equipment.

contaminated water: Any body of water that contains biological, chemical, or nuclear materials that are potentially harmful to human life.

core temperature: The internal temperature of the human body. Normally, this will be 98.6 degrees F at rest.

crushed neoprene: A synthetic foam neoprene material that has been deliberately collapsed under pressure. This process is patented by DUI.

d

decontamination: The process of cleaning a diver and his equipment after exposure to contaminated water.

Glossary of Dry Suit Diving Terms

denier: A measurement of the weight and thickness of a fabric.

Desco: A manufacturer of full face masks and diving helmets. Their products are referred to by the company name.

Doppler flow meter: An electronic device that can be attached to a diver's body to detect bubbles of inert gas in the diver's blood stream. Dopplers are commonly used to study decompression and dive computer performance.

diving bell: A spherical or cylindrical steel pressure chamber that can be lowered into the sea to transport divers to depth in a temperature and pressure controlled environment. Diving bells are used for bounce and saturation diving in commercial, scientific, and military operations.

e

encapsulation: Any system that is designed to completely isolate and protect a person from his/her surrounding environment. A dry suit, dry gloves, and diving helmet can be mated together to protect a diver from microscopic biological organisms that may be present in the water.

EPDM: The material used in the manufacture of many vulcanized rubber dry suits. EPDM is an additive used in the compounding of the rubber.

f

flaring: A technique used to slow a diver's ascent through the water. The diver arches his back, holds his arms out parallel to the surface, and holds his fin blades parallel to the surface, too. The increased drag caused by this posture will slow, but not stop, an uncontrolled ascent.

flashlight method: A method of locating dry suit leaks. Take your dry suit into a darkened room, put a flashlight inside the suit and turn it on. Shine the flashlight toward the outside of the suit in the area of the suspected puncture. The light should shine through the hole and make the leak easy to find.

full face masks: Any diving mask designed to cover the diver's eyes, nose, and mouth. The mask does not cover the back of the diver's head or ears.

h

haz-mat: A non-technical term that denotes any operation or incident that involves hazardous chemicals, biological organisms, or nuclear contamination. May also be used to refer to training or equipment associated with hazardous materials.

hazardous materials: Any material that is potentially dangerous to the human body or to other biological organisms.

heavy gear: Old style commercial diving equipment that includes rubberized canvas suit and a tinned copper helmet. The helmet and the suit are open to each other.

Glossary of Dry Suit Diving Terms

hot water suit: A diving suit that is connected to a surface supply of hot water via a hose. Hot water is pumped into the suit and is distributed throughout the suit by a series of tubes.

hot zone: The center of a contaminated site where the concentration of contaminants is the highest.

hydrophobic: Any material that repels water. Dry suit undergarments made of Thinsulate® are hydrophobic.

Hypalon: A material that is very resistant to chemicals. Hypalon can be used to make dry suits, although it is not a commonly used material.

hypothermia: A physiological cindition where the human core temperature drops to an unacceptably low level. Hypothermia can cause death if not corrected.

I

Incident command supervisor: The supervisor in charge of any event that may be dangerous to the safety of the public. An incident command supervisor is usually appointed to manage the various agencies that may respond to a hazardous materials incident.

insulation strategy: A diver's predetermined plan for how to deal with particular ranges of water temperature.

l

latex: A natural rubber compound that is used to manufacture dry suit wrist and neck seals.

layering: An insulation strategy where the diver wears multiple layers of undergarments that can be added or removed according to the diver's activity level and the water temperature.

"Level A" protection: The highest level of protection for working in a contaminated environment. Level A protection includes an encapsulating suit with self-contained or hose supplied breathing apparatus. Underwater this might be comparable to a dry suit, mating gloves, and a dry helmet with surface supplied breathing air.

"Level B" protection: A lower level of protection for working in contaminated environments than Level A. For topside work this includes a hooded splash suit with self-contained breathing apparatus. Underwater this might be comparable to a dry suit, mating gloves, and a full face mask.

"Level C" protection: A minimum level of protection for a hazardous environment. For topside applications this includes a hooded suit for skin protection and an air purifying cannister.

n

Naval Surface Weapons Center: A Navy testing facility where dry suit research has been performed. The center is located in Virginia.

Glossary of Dry Suit Diving Terms

o

open cell foam: A type of material that has sponge cells that are open to each other. This material has been used for dry suit underwear. The material does not compress because air can move freely through the material.

p

Passive Diver Thermal Protection System: The Navy term for the dry suit system that was developed during the 1980's. The abbreviation for this system is the PDTPS. As the name implies, there is no external heat source.

PDTPS: See Passive Diver Thermal Protection System.

permeation: The ability of a chemical to move through a material at the molecular level.

polluted water: Any body of water that contains contaminants that are harmful to the human body. See contaminated water.

pressure proof zipper: A zipper that seals with a rubber sealing surface and holds back both water and air under pressure. A dry suit zipper is a pressure proof zipper.

r

respiratory heat loss: Heat that is lost from the body from the lungs. In cold water, each time a scuba diver exhales underwater body heat and moisture will be lost.

s

saturation diving: A diving mode where the diver lives under pressure and becomes completely saturated with inert gas for a specific depth. Complete saturation is considered to occur after the diver has been under pressure for 24 hours. Once the diver is saturated, his decompression obligation is the same whether he has been underwater for one day or two months.

SEALAB: The Navy program where divers spent extended periods living underwater in a habitat. SEALAB I was stationed off Bermuda in 1964. SEALAB II was stationed off La Jolla, California in 1965. SEALAB III was stationed off San Clemente Island in California in 1968 but was aborted shortly after launch.

splash suit: A suit designed to protect a person on the surface from splashes of toxic chemicals. Splash suits are usually only used with less hazardous chemicals.

squeeze: A pressure related injury. Squeezes occur when there is insufficient air pressure in closed spaces in or around the body. Early dry suits were not equipped with inflator valves and divers frequently had their skin pinched in the folds of the suits. These injuries produced blisters on the diver's skin.

standby diver: The diver who is next in line to dive on a commercial diving job. Normally, the standby diver is completely dressed in and ready to go to the assistance of the diver on the bottom.

Glossary of Dry Suit Diving Terms

SuperLite-17®: A popular commercial diving helmet developed by the diving inventors Bev Morgan and Bob Kirby. The helmet is manufactured by Diving Systems International in Santa Barbara, CA.

Supersuit: A foam neoprene dry suit manufactured by O'Neill and popular during the 1970's.

t

tender: A commercial diver's apprentice. A tender is normally a diver in training. The tender is responsible for "tending" to the diver's needs and "tending" the surface supplied diver's air hose.

Texas Research Institute: A "think tank" that performs many different testing programs for the military and private industry.

thermal protection: Equipment worn to protect a human from the effects of heat or cold.

Thinsulate® A synthetic fiber developed by the 3M company to be used as insulation in clothing.

topside air supply: An air supply used for commercial diving, where the air is sent to a diver wearing a helmet or full face mask via hose. A topside air supply may be either a low pressure compressor or a high pressure system with a regulator.

TLS material: A popular dry suit material. TLS material was originally developed for use in chemical warfare suits.

tube suit: A suit that is specially constructed with a network of tubes to distribute heated or chilled water to all parts of the wearer's body to control body temperature. The tube suit is normally worn under a dry suit. The tubes are sealed, the diver is kept dry and the water is recirculated and reheated.

tunnel entry suit: A dry suit with an opening in the chest or back to allow a diver to get into the suit. Once the diver is inside, the tube or "tunnel" is gathered together and closed off with a clamp or large rubber band.

Turbo hood: A patented dry suit hood developed by Scandinavian inventors Stig Insulan and Jorn Stubdal. The hood is actually a double hood, with a thin latex liner and an outer layer of vulcanized rubber.

u

underpressure: A phenomenon common to all dry suits. The part of your body that is deepest will always have more pressure on it than the part of your body that is shallowest. In a dry suit, the air will always shift to the uppermost part of the suit. The increased pressure felt on the lowest part of your body is known as an underpressure.

unearned fatigue: fatigue that results from diving in cold water, even if you have done very little swimming or other physical activity.

Glossary of Dry Suit Diving Terms

Unisuit: One of the first commercially successful dry suits to use a waterproof zipper and a suit inflator system.

urethane: A synthetic material that is used as a waterproof backing in many types of dry suits.

V

vasoconstriction: A physiological reaction to cold where the human body shuts down the blood flow to the skin and extremities.

ventricular fibrillation: A condition where the heart goes into an irregular, uncoordinated beat that will not circulate blood. This condition will lead to death if not corrected.

viton/chlorobutyl: A combination of synthetic materials that is very resistant to toxic chemicals. This material is under investigation by the U.S. Navy for use in contaminated water diving suits.

vulcanized rubber: Rubber that has been treated under heat and pressure to improve its characteristics in terms of stretch, ozone resistance, and durability.

W

warm neck collar: A special dry suit collar that is used in conjunction with a wet suit hood with a cold water bib. The bib on the hood is tucked under the warm neck collar to reduce water circulation.

wrist valves: A small exhaust valve for a dry suit that may be mounted on the wrist or ankle. These valves have no variable pressure setting, but will exhaust any time the internal pressure of the suit exceeds the external pressure at that particular body location.

Bibliography

Adsolfson, J., Sperling, L., and Gustavsson, M. Hand protection. In *Arctic Underwater Operations: Medical and Operational Aspects of Diving Activities in Arctic Conditions*. Rey, L. (editor). Graham and Trotman, Worcester, England, 1985, pgs. 237-254.

Anonymous. Thinsulate: 3M proves that thin can be warm. In *Business Week Magazine*, January, 1979.

Audet, N., Orner, G., and Zupferman, Z. Thermal insulation materials for diver's underwear garment. In *Proceedings Hyperbaric Diving Systems and Thermal Protection*. American Society of Mechanical Engineers, New York, NY, 1978, pgs. 133-149.

Bachrach, A., and Egstrom, G. *Stress and Performance in Diving*. Best Publishing, San Pedro, CA, 1987, pgs. 31-33, 149-154.

Baldwin, M. The survival suit. In *Oceans Magazine*, Vol. 19, September/October, 1986, pgs. 40-45.

Barsky, S. *The Dry Suit Diving Manual*. Marine Marketing and Consulting, Santa Barbara, CA, 1988.

Barsky, S. *Diving in High Risk Environments*. Dive Rescue International, Inc., Ft. Collins, CO, 1990.

Barsky, S., and Heine, J. Observations of flooded dry suit buoyancy characteristics. In *Advances in Underwater Science '88: Proceedings of the American Academy of Underwater Sciences*, Lang, M. (editor). American Academy of Underwater Sciences, Costa Mesa, CA, 1988, pgs. 1-11.

Baumgardner, J., Graves, D., Neufeld, G., and Quinn, J. Gas flux through human skin: effect of temperature, stripping, and inspired tension. In *Journal of Applied Physiology*, 1985, pgs. 1536-1545.

Bradner, H. Personal Memorandum to Dr. L.C. Marshall. University of California, Berkeley, June, 1951.

Bridgman, S. Thermal status of antarctic divers. In *Aviation, Space, and Environmental Medicine*, September, 1990, pgs. 795-800.

Burnet, H., Lucciano, M., and Jammes, Y. Respiratory effects of cold-gas breathing in humans under hyperbaric environment. In *Respiration Physiology*, Vol. 81,1990, pgs. 413-424.

Choi, J., Park, Y., Park, Y., Kim, J., Yeon, D., Kang, D., Rennie, D., and Hong, S. Effect of wearing gloves on the thermal balance of Korean women wet-suit divers in cold water. In *Undersea Biomedical Reports*, Vol. 15, No. 3, 1988, pgs. 155-164.

Coolbaugh, J., Daily, O., Joseph, S., and Colwell, R. Bacterial contamination of divers during training exercises in coastal waters. *Marine Technology Society Journal*, Washington, DC, Vol. 15, No. 2, 1981, pgs. 15-22.

Cousteau, J. *World Without Sun*. Harper & Row, New York, 1964.

Cousteau, J., and Dumas, F. *The Silent World*. Harper & Row, New York, 1953.

Dunford, R., and Hayward, J. Venuous gas bubble production following cold stress during a no-decompression dive. In *Undersea Biomedical Research*, Vol. 8, No. 1, March, 1981, pgs. 41-49.

Bibliography

Egstrom, G. Thermal problems in diving. In *Proceedings from the Working Diver Symposium 1978.* Marine Technology Society, Washington, DC, 1978. pgs. 35–44.

Egstrom, G., Weltman, G., Cuccaro, W., and Willis, M. *Underwater Work Tolerance and Performance.* Department of the Navy, Office of Naval Research, 1973.

Flynn, E. New approaches to the solution of diving medical problems. In the *Marine Technology Society Journal*, Vol. 23, No. 4, December, 1989, pgs. 12–18.

Glowe, D. Final Report: *Chemical Compatability Testing of Diving Related Materials.* Prepared for Naval Surface Weapons Center. Prepared by Texas Research Institute, Austin, TX, 1983.

Graham, T. Thermal, metabolic, and cardiovascular changes in men and women during cold stress. In *Medicine and Science in Sports and Exercise,* American College of Sports Medicine, Vol. 20, No. 5, 1988, pgs. 185–192.

Hackett, M. Desert diving: the ICSURT story, In *The Backup: Official Publication of the California Reserve Peace Officers Association,* Trident Media, Santa Ana, CA, Vol. 8, No. 4, 1988, pgs. 10–15.

Hanna, J., and Hong, S. Critical water temperature and effective insulation in scuba divers in Hawaii. In *Journal of Applied Physiology,* 1972, Vol. 33, No. 6, pgs. 770–773.

Haux, G. *Subsea Manned Engineering.* Bailliere Tindall, London, England, 1982, pgs. 138, 166, 380.

Hayes, P. Thermal protection equipment. In *Arctic Underwater Operations: Medical and Operational Aspects of Diving Activities in Arctic Conditions.* Rey, L.(editor). Graham and Trotman, Worcester, England, 1985, pgs. 193–216.

Hoffman, R. and Pozos, R. Experimental hypothermia and cold perception. In *Aviation Space, and Environmental Medicine,* October, 1989, pgs. 964–969.

Hoke, B., Jackson, B., Alexander, J., and Flyn, E. Respiratory heat loss and pulmonary functions during cold gas breathing at high pressures. In *Underwater Physiology,* Lambertsen, C. (editor). Bethesda, MD: FASEB, 1976, pgs. 725–740.

Johnson, A. Police profile: HPD dive team. In *Badge and Gun: Magazine of the Houston Police Officers Association,* Houston, TX Vol. 2, No. 10, 1986.

Keatinge, W. Thermal balance. In *Arctic Underwater Operations: Medical and Operational Aspects of Diving Activities in Arctic Conditions.* Rey, L. (editor). Graham and Trotman, Worcester, England, 1985, pgs. 19–28.

Kuehn, L. Medical and physiological problems. In *Arctic Underwater Operations: Medical and Operational Aspects of Diving Activities in Arctic Conditions.* Rey, L. (editor). Graham and Trotman, Worcester, England, 1985, pgs. 7–18.

Kuehn, L., and Ackles, K. Thermal exposure limits for divers. In proceedings *Hyperbaric Diving Systems and Thermal Protection. American Society of Mechanical Engineers,* New York, NY, 1978, pgs. 39–53.

Bibliography

Lomax, P. Environmental stress. In *Arctic Underwater Operations: Medical and Operational Aspects of Diving Activities in Arctic Conditions*. Rey, L. (editor). Graham and Trotman, Worcester, England, 1985, pgs. 29-40.

Long, R. Dive suit buoyancy control problems and solutions. In *Proceedings of the Biomechanics of Safe Ascents Workshop*. Egstrom, G. and Lang, M. (editors). American Academy of Underwater Sciences, Costa Mesa, CA, 1989, pgs. 103-110.

Manson, H. What a diving team needs to know about hypothermia. In *Arctic Underwater Operations: Medical and Operational Aspects of Diving Activities in Arctic Conditions*. Rey, Louis (editor). Graham and Trotman, Worcester, England, 1985, pgs. 255-262.

Mekjavic, I., and Kakitsuba, N. Effects of peripheral temperature on the formation of venuous gas bubbles. In *Undersea Biomedical Research*, Vol. 16, No. 5, 1989, pgs. 391-401.

Middleton, J. *Evaluation of Poseidon Unisuit and O'Neill Supersuit Systems*. Navy Experimental Diving Unit, Report No. 4-79, January, 1979

Ministry of Defense. *Specifications for Double Textured Nylon with Butyl Rubber Interply,* Publication No. UK/SC/4676. Stores and Clothing Research and Development Establishment, Colchester, England, January, 1981.

Monji, K., Nakashima, K., Sogabe, Y., Miki, K., Tajima, F., and Shiraki, K. Changes in insulation in wetsuits during repetitive exposure to pressure. In *Undersea Biomedical Research*, Vol. 16, No. 4, 1989, pgs. 313-319.

Muza, S., Young, A., Sawka, M., Bogart, J. and Pandolf, K. Respiratory and cardiovascular responses to cold stress following repeated cold water immersion. In *Undersea Biomedical Research*, Vol. 15, No. 3, 1988, pgs. 165-178.

Netherby, S. Thinsulate: A new way to insulate. In *Field and Stream Magazine*, June, 1979.

Nuckols, M. Thermal considerations in the design of diver's suits. In Proceedings *Hyperbaric Diving Systems and Thermal Protection*. American Society of Mechanical Engineers, New York, NY, 1978, pgs. 83-101.

Nunnely, S. Heat, Cold, hard work, and the woman diver. In symposium proceedings, *Women in Diving, 35th UHMS Workshop*. Undersea Hyperbaric Medical Society, April, 1987, pgs. 35-44.

Park, Y., Iwamoto, F., Miki, K., Park, Y., and Shiraki, K. Effect of pressure on thermal insulation in humans wearing wet suits. In *Journal of Applied Physiology*, 1988, pgs, 1916-1922

Pendergast, D. The effect of body cooling on oxygen transport during exercise. In *Medicine and Science in Sports and Exercise*, American College of Sports Medicine, Vol. 20, No. 5, 1988, pgs. 171-176.

Penzias, W. and Goodman, M. *Man Beneath the Sea: A Review of Underwater Ocean Engineering*.Wiley Interscience, New York, 1973 pgs. 586-628.

Bibliography

Pohlman, T. Development of a chemical warfare dive suit (CWPDS) for United States Navy diving in contaminated water. In *Chemical Protective Clothing Performance in Chemical Emergency Response*, American Society for Testing Materials, Perkins, J. and Stull, J. (editors), Philadelphia, PA, 1989, pgs. 174-184.

Radloff, R., and Helmreich, R. *Groups Under Stress: Psychological Performance in SEALAB II.* Aplleton-Century-Crofts, New York, 1968.

Reins, D. and Shampine, J. Evaluation of heat loss from Navy divers' wet suit. Navy Clothing and Textile Research Unit, Natick, MA. Technical Report No. 102, July, 1972.

Rennie, D. Tissue heat transfer in water: lessons from the Korean divers. In *Medicine and Science in Sports and Exercise*, American College of Sports Medicine, Vol. 20, No. 5, 1988, pgs. 177-184.

Scott, J. Cold comfort: wetsuit inventor left with a warm feeling but no money. In *Los Angeles Times*, January 10, 1988, Section J, pgs. 1, 6.

Shiraki, K., Sueko, S, and Hong, S. Thermal problems associated with diving in cold water. In the *Marine Technology Society Journal*, Vol. 23, No. 4, December, 1989, pgs. 72-81.

Sterba, J. , Hanson, R. , and Stiglich, J. *Insulation, Compressibility, and Absorbency of Dry Suit Undergarments.* Navy Experimental Diving Unit, NEDU Report No. 10-89, August, 1989.

Stinton, R. Dry suit valves and performance. In *Proceedings of the Biomechanics of Safe Ascents Workshop.* Egstrom, G. and Lang, M. (editors) American Academy of Underwater Sciences, Costa Mesa, CA, 1989, pgs. 111-122.

Toner, M., Holden, W., Foley, M., Bogart, J., and Pandolf, K. Influence of clothing and body-fat insulation on thermal adjustments to cold-water stress. In *Aviation, Space, and Environmental Medicine*, October, 1989, pgs. 957-963.

Traver, R. *Manual of Practice for Marine Safety Officers and On-Scene Coordinators Involved in Chemically and/or Biologically Contaminated Underwater Operations (Interim Protocol).* Hazardous Waste Engineering Research Laboratory, Office of Research and Development, U.S. Environmental Protection Agency, Cincinnati, OH, 1984.

Vangaard, L. Cold-induced changes. In *Arctic Underwater Operations: Medical and Operational Aspects of Diving Activities in Arctic Conditions.* Rey, L. (editor). Graham and Trotman, Worcester, England, 1985, pgs. 41-48.

Virr, L. Mechanical design and operation of thermal protection equipment. In *Arctic Underwater Operations: Medical and Operational Aspects of Diving Activities in Arctic Conditions.* Rey, Louis (editor). Graham and Trotman, Worcester, England, 1985, pgs. 217-236.

Wattenberger, J., and Breckenridge, J. Dry suit insulation characteristics under hyperbaric conditions. In Proceedings *Hyperbaric Diving Systems and Thermal Protection.* American Society of Mechanical Engineers, New York, NY, 1978, pgs. 101-117.

Bibliography

Weathersby, P., Survanshi, S., and Nishi, R. Relative decompression risk of dry and wet chamber air dives. In *Undersea Biomedical Research*, Vol. 17, No. 4, 1990, pgs. 333-352.

Webb, P. Thermal problems. In *The Physiology and Medicine of Diving*, Bennett, P., Elliott, D. (editors) , Bailliere Tindall, London, England, 1982, pgs. 297-318.

Weinberg, R. and Thalman, E. Effects of hand and foot heating on diver thermal balance. Naval Medical Research Institute, Protocol 88-04, Draft Revision April 1990.

Whang, J., Quinn, J., Graves, D., Neufield, G. Permeation of inert gases through human skin: modeling the effect of skin blood flow. In *Journal of Applied Physiology*, 1989, pgs. 1670-1682.

Wolf, A., Coleshaw, S., Newstead, C., and Keatinge, W. Heat exchanges in wet suits. In *Journal of Applied Physiology*, 1985, pgs. 770-777.

Index

Symbols

A

B

C

Index

Index

Index

Index

Index

Index

Index

Index

W

Index